SHRUBS

SHRUBS

Richard Bird

Photography by Jonathan Buckley

LORENZ BOOKS

First published in 1998 by Lorenz Books
27 West 20th Street, New York, NY 10011

LORENZ BOOKS are available for bulk purchase for sales promotion and for
premium use. For details, write or call the sales director,
Lorenz Books, 27 West 20th Street, New York, NY 10011;
(800) 354-9657

Lorenz Books is an imprint of
Anness Publishing Limited

ISBN 1 85967 677 4

Publisher: Joanna Lorenz
Project Editor: Alison Macfarlane
Editor: Deborah Savage
Designer: Caroline Reeves
Photographer: Jonathan Buckley
Illustrator: Nicky Cooney

Printed in Hong Kong

1 3 5 7 9 10 8 6 4 2

CONTENTS

Introduction	**6**
TECHNIQUES	**8**
DESIGNING A BORDER	**32**
CHOOSING SHRUBS	**40**
SHRUBS FOR ALL SEASONS	**74**
Plant List	**92**
Index	**94**
Acknowledgements	**96**

INTRODUCTION

Shrubs are the mainstay of our gardens; a garden without them would be inconceivable. They not only provide the obvious things, such as colour, both in their flowers and their foliage, but structure, shape, texture and scent. They also provide a natural habitat for wildlife, offering food and shelter as well as nesting sites.

Shrubs also have the great advantage that they are not difficult to look after. On the whole, apart from a little pruning and perhaps some mulching, little else is required. Indeed, many shrubs can be more or less left to their own devices.

Gardening with shrubs can be a great adventure as there are so many to choose from. It is a good idea to draw up a plan, so that when you come to planting you know exactly what you want. Ideas can be obtained from books or from looking at other gardens. Jot down the names of shrubs you like and combinations that are particularly appealing. Research of this kind is always part of the fun of gardening, as is sitting down and making sketches of what you want to create.

In this book we have tried to show a wide range of shrubs, their uses and how to grow them. Equipped with this knowledge, the gardener can look forward to many hours of happy gardening and satisfaction in the results of his or her labour.

Right: Cotinus coggyria *with sun shining through its leaves.*

TECHNIQUES

Soil Preparation

One of the most important of all gardening techniques is soil preparation. It is the foundation of all future growth and success. Neglect it and you are likely to face an uphill battle to produce any plants worth having.

REMOVING THE WEEDS

There are several important stages. The first is to rid the ground of weeds. Annual weeds are a nuisance but no more than this and, over a period, they will slowly be eliminated as their seed store in the ground is reduced. The real problem is persistent perennial weeds. In soft, friable soils, these can be removed by hand as the soil is dug. In heavier conditions, the only sure way is to use a chemical weedkiller. Modern herbicides are safe to use as long as the instructions on the packet are rigorously followed. If used properly, the weeds will be killed and, with good maintenance, there should be no need to use herbicides again.

CONDITIONING THE SOIL

It is important to improve the condition of the soil before you start to plant. Dig as much well-rotted organic material as possible into the soil. This will not only help break down the soil but will also provide nutrients for the shrubs' growth. It will also help the soil to provide a reservoir of moisture down around the shrubs' roots. The best organic material is garden compost. This can be prepared by piling up waste matter, such as leaves, the stems and dead flowers of herbaceous material, non-invasive weeds and grass clippings, together with uncooked waste from the kitchen, such as peelings, and allowing them to break down naturally. Woody stems, such as prunings and hedge clippings, can be added, as long as they have been allowed to rot down first. Other material can be obtained from outside the garden: farmyard manure, old mushroom compost and composted bark are all invaluable.

SOIL CONDITIONERS

Chipped or composted bark – little nutritional value, but good mulch.
Farmyard manure – rich in nutrients, but often contains weed seed. Good conditioner.
Garden compost – composted garden waste. Good nutrient value and good conditioner.
Leaf mould – composted leaves. Good nutritional value. Excellent conditioner and mulch.
Peat – not very suitable as it breaks down too quickly and has little nutritional value.
Seaweed – rich in minerals. Good conditioner.
Spent hops – brewery waste. Some nutritional value, good mulch and conditioner.
Spent mushroom compost – good mulch. Contains chalk or lime.

MAKING A NEW BED

1 Choose the site of the bed and mark out its shape. This can be done with a hosepipe (garden hose), moving it around until you have the shape you want. Then dig around it with a spade, lawn edger or hoe.

2 For a circular bed, place a post in the centre of the proposed circle and tie a piece of string to it. Attach a sharp stick or tool at the radius (half the diameter) of the circle and, with the string pulled taut, scribe a circle around the central post. An alternative is to tie a bottle filled with sand to the string and allow the sand to trickle out as you move the bottle round the circle.

3 If the grass contains pernicious and persistent weeds, remove them before digging. The only sure way is to kill them with a herbicide. If the surrounding grass is full of such weeds, these should also be killed or they will soon encroach on the bed.

4 With many lawn grasses, it will not be necessary to use herbicide; simply skim off the surface grass and dig out any roots that remain.

5 Dig the soil, removing any weeds and stones. If possible, double dig the soil, breaking up the lower spit (spade's depth) but not bringing this soil to the surface.

6 Mix plenty of organic material into both layers of the soil, but especially the bottom layer, to encourage the roots to grow deeply.

7 If possible, leave the bed to weather for a few months after digging; then remove any residual weeds that have appeared. When you are ready to plant, add some well-rotted compost or ready-prepared soil conditioner to the soil and lightly fork it in. The weather should have broken the soil down to a certain extent, but the rain will also have compacted it. Lightly fork it over to loosen the soil, break down any lumps and work in any soil conditioner.

8 Rake over the soil, to give it its final tilth, creating an even level over the bed but with a channel round the edge to facilitate trimming the edge of the lawn.

Right: Escallonia 'Gwendolyn Anley' covered in flower. To grow healthy plants that are both vigorous and floriferous all weeds should be removed and the condition of the soil should be improved.

Planting Shrubs

There is nothing difficult about planting a shrub, except possibly making the decision as to where to plant it. One thing that must always be borne in mind is that shrubs *do* grow, and it is a common mistake to underestimate by how much. The result is that shrubs are often planted too close together and then the gardener is faced with the heart-rending decision as to which to dig out so that the others can continue to grow. Avoid this by finding out how big the plant will grow and allowing for this when planting. This means there will be gaps between the shrubs for the first few years but these can be temporarily filled with herbaceous perennials and annuals.

PLANTING CARE

If you are planting more than one shrub at a time, stand them all, still in their pots, on the bed in the places where you wish to plant them, so that you can check that they will all fit in and that the arrangement is a good one. Make any adjustments before you begin to plant, as it does the shrubs no good to be dug up and replanted several times because you have put them in the wrong place.

The actual planting is not a difficult process but looking after the plant once it is planted is important. Water it well until it becomes established. If the site is a windy one, protect either the whole bed or individual shrubs with windbreak netting, until they are firmly established. In really hot weather, light shading will help relieve stress on the plant as its new roots struggle to get enough moisture to supply the rapidly transpiring leaves.

Other aspects to consider in positioning shrubs are discussed elsewhere in the book.

PLANTING TIMES

The recommended time for planting shrubs is at any time between autumn and early spring provided that the weather allows you to do so. Planting should not take place if the weather is too wet or too cold or if the ground is waterlogged or frozen.

However this advice is basically for bare-rooted plants – that is, those dug up from nursery beds. Although container-grown plants are easier to establish if planted at the same time, it is possible to plant out at any time of the year as long as the rootball is not disturbed. If planting takes place in the summer, then avoid doing it during very hot or dry weather. The plants will need constant watering and protection from the effects of drying winds and strong sun.

1 Before you start planting, check that the plant has been watered. If not, give it a thorough soaking, preferably at least an hour before planting.

2 If the soil has not been recently prepared, fork it over, removing any weeds. Add a slow-release fertilizer, such as bonemeal, wearing rubber or vinyl gloves if required, and fork this in.

3 Dig the hole, preferably much wider than the rootball of the shrub. Place the plant, still in its pot, in the hole and check that the hole is deep enough by placing a stick or cane across the hole: the top of the pot should align with the top of the soil Adjust the depth of the hole accordingly.

4 Remove the plant from its pot, being careful not to disturb the rootball. If it is in a plastic bag, cut the bag away rather than trying to pull it off. Place the shrub in the hole and pull the earth back around it. Firm the soil down well around the plant with the heel of your boot and water well.

5 Finally, mulch all around the shrub, covering the soil with 7.5–10 cm (3–4 in) of bark or similar material. This will not only help to preserve the moisture but will also help to prevent weeds from germinating.

Right: White frothy mounds of flowers are produced by Spiraea *'Arguta' during the spring. Since it produces its flowers before many other shrubs come into leaf, it can be planted towards the back of the border where it will show up while in flower but then merge into the background for the rest of the year when it is not so striking.*

Moving a Shrub

The ideal, when planting shrubs, is to place them in the right position first time round, but, occasionally, it becomes necessary to move one. If the shrub has only been in the ground a few weeks, this is not too much of a problem: simply dig around the plant, lifting it with as big a ball of earth as possible on the spade and move it to a ready-prepared new hole. Moving a well-established shrub requires more thought and planning.

1 If possible, root-prune the shrub a few months before moving, to encourage the formation of new fibrous roots. Water the plant well the day before moving it.

MOVING A WELL-ESTABLISHED SHRUB TO A NEW HOME

If the move is part of a long-term plan, there may well be time to root-prune the shrub first, a few months before you intend to move it. This involves digging a trench or simply slicing a sharp spade into the soil around the shrub, to sever the roots. This encourages the shrub to produce more fibrous feeding roots on the remaining roots and makes it easier for it to become established once it is moved.

Once you have moved the shrub, keep it well-watered and, as with all newly-planted shrubs, if it is in a windy situation, protect it with windbreak netting to prevent excessive transpiration. Shrubs that have been moved are likely to be vulnerable to wind-rock and so it is important to stake them firmly.

A shrub with a large ball of earth around its roots is a very heavy and unwieldy object to move. This can be a recipe for a back injury, so be very careful. Always get somebody to help, if possible. This will also ensure you don't drop the plant, causing the soil around the roots to drop off, which makes it far more difficult to re-establish the plant.

2 Dig a trench around the plant, leaving a rootball that two people can comfortably lift. Sever any roots you encounter to release the rootball.

3 Dig under the shrub, cutting through any tap roots that hold it in place.

4 Rock the plant to one side and insert some hessian (burlap) sacking or strong plastic sheeting as far under the plant as you can. Push several folds of material under the rootball.

5 Rock it in the opposite direction and pull the hessian sacking or plastic sheeting through, so that it is completely under the plant.

6 Pull the sheeting round the rootball so that it completely encloses the soil and tie it firmly around the neck of the plant. The shrub is now ready to move. If it is a small plant, one person may be able to lift it out of the hole and transfer it to its new site.

7 If the plant plus the soil is heavy, it is best moved by two people. This can be made much easier by tying a bar of wood or metal to the trunk of the shrub or to the sacking. With one person on each end, lift the shrub out of the hole.

8 Prepare the ground and hole as for a new shrub and lower the transplanted shrub into it. Follow the reverse procedure, unwrapping and removing the sheeting from the rootball. Ensure the plant is in the right position and refill the hole.

Right: *Once the shrub has been replanted in its new position, water it thoroughly and mulch the soil around it. In more exposed positions place netting round it to prevent winds from drying the plant out and scorching it. It may also need protection from fierce sun. Moving a shrub in autumn or winter, as long as it is not too cold or wet, will allow it to become established in time for its first summer.*

Staking a Shrub

In a well protected garden or in a border where a new shrub is surrounded by other supportive shrubs or plants, it may well be unnecessary to stake, but where the wind is likely to catch a shrub it is important to stake it until it is established.

SHORT AND TALL STAKING

The aim of staking a shrub is to allow the new roots to move out into the soil while anchoring the plant firmly. If the wind rocks the plant, the ball of soil that came with the plant is likely to move as well, severing the new roots that are trying to spread out into the surrounding soil.

The modern technique for staking trees and shrubs is to ensure that the base of the shrub is firmly anchored, preventing the rootball from moving, while the top is free to move in the wind, which will strengthen it. Thus, only a short stake is required, with a single tie about 25 cm (10 in) or so above the ground. If the shrub is top-heavy – for example, a standard rose – it is important to use a taller stake and tie it in two places, or the top of the shrub may well snap off. Unlike other forms of staking, this support should be left in place rather than removed once the shrub is established.

Both short and tall staking is best done when first planting the shrub so that the roots can be seen. If the stake is knocked in afterwards it is likely to sever unseen roots. If it becomes necessary to stake a mature or already-planted shrub, use two stakes set some way out on either side of the shrub, with a crossbar to tie the stems to.

USEFUL SUPPORTS

A number of items can be used as stakes for shrubs. You can buy a variety of specially-designed plastic or wire supports from your local garden centre; alternatively, twiggy sticks pushed into the ground around a plant can be effective. Use short garden canes for fragile plants, tall canes for plants with tall, flowering stems and thicker pieces of wood for shrubs that need a stronger or more permanent means of support.

STAKING A STANDARD SHRUB

1 For a standard shrub, make sure you use a strong stake. It should be of a rot-resistant wood or one that has been treated with preservative. Firmly place the stake in the planting hole, knocking it into the soil so that it cannot move.

2 Plant the shrub, pushing the rootball up against the stake, so that the stem and stake are approximately 7.5–10 cm (3–4 in) apart.

3 Firm the soil down around the plant with the heel of your boot.

4 Although it is possible to use string, a proper rose or tree tie provides the best support. Fix the lower one 15 cm (6 in) above the soil.

5 Then fix the second tie near the top of the stake, just below the head of the standard shrub.

6 Water the ground around the plant thoroughly and mulch with a chipped bark or similar material.

Right: *Regularly check the ties, to make certain they are not too tight; otherwise they will begin to cut into the wood as the stems of the shrub increase in girth.*

Principles of Pruning

Pruning is the one thing that gardeners worry about more than anything else. The upshot is that many are frightened to do any pruning, feeling that it is probably best to leave things alone. While this may work with some shrubs, it is best to get into the habit of regularly checking all shrubs and pruning those that need it. Certainly, the shrubs will benefit from this.

BASIC PRUNING

With a little practice, pruning is not as difficult a task as many people fear. There are several basic elements to pruning and taking them one step at a time makes the whole process much clearer and easier to deal with.

The first step is to remove all dead wood. This opens up the shrub and makes it easier to see what is happening. The second is to remove any diseased wood. Both of these are easy steps as it is usually not difficult to decide what to remove.

The second stage is more difficult but becomes much easier with practice. This is to remove any weak wood from the shrub and to cut off stems that cross or rub other ones.

Finally, in order to keep a shrub vigorous it is important to encourage new growth. The way to do this is to select a few of the oldest stems and remove them. Up to a third of the shrub can be removed at any one time. The pruning is now complete, except for a final check to see if there are any stems that seem out of place and need removing; in other words just tidy up the plant to make certain that it has an attractive shape.

GOOD CUTS

1 A good pruning cut is made just above a strong bud, about 3 mm (⅛ in) above the bud. It should be a slanting cut, with the higher end above the bud. The bud should generally be outward bound from the plant rather than inward; the latter will throw its shoot into the plant, crossing and rubbing against others, which should be avoided. This is an easy technique and you can practise it on any stem.

2 If the stem has buds or leaves opposite each other, make the cut horizontal, again about 3 mm (⅛ in) above the buds.

BASIC PRUNING CUTS FOR THICKER BRANCHES

For thicker branches, use a saw rather than attempting to use a pair of secateurs (pruners). A sharp pruning saw is better than a wood-working saw.

The major problem of cutting thicker stems is that they usually have a considerable weight. If cut straight through, this weight bends the stem before the cut has been completed, tearing the branch below the cut back to the main stem or trunk. The following technique avoids this. It is no longer considered necessary to paint large cuts to protect them.

1 Choose a point 5 cm (2 in) or more away from the position of the final cut and make a saw cut from beneath the branch. Continue until you are about halfway through or until the weight of the branch begins to bind on the saw.

2 Next, make a downward cut from the top of the branch about 2.5 cm (1 in) or so on the outside of the first cut. When the saw has cut to level with the first cut, the weight of the branch is likely to make the branch split or tear along to the first cut.

3 Sawing from above, cut through the branch at the desired point. Now you have removed most of the weight of the branch, it should be possible to cut cleanly through the branch and thus finish the pruning.

BAD CUTS

3 Always use a sharp pair of secateurs (pruners). Blunt ones will produce a ragged or bruised cut, which is likely to introduce disease into the plant.

4 Do not cut too far above a bud. The piece of stem above the bud is likely to die back and the stem may well die back even further, causing the loss of the whole stem.

5 Do not cut too close to the bud otherwise the bud might be damaged by the secateurs or disease might enter. Too close a cut is likely to cause the stem to die back to the next bud.

6 It is bad practice to slope the cut towards the bud as this makes the stem above the bud too long, which is likely to cause dieback. It also sheds rain on to the bud, which may cause problems.

DECIDING WHEN TO PRUNE

Perhaps the most difficult aspect of pruning is deciding when to do it. Gardeners worry that if they do it at the wrong time they might kill the plant. This is possible but unlikely. The worst that usually happens is that you cut off all the stems that will produce the year's flowers and so you miss a season. As a rule of thumb, most shrubs need to be pruned immediately after they have flowered, so that they have time to produce new mature stems by the time they need to flower again.

Right: *The beautiful* Hydrangea *'Ayesha' needs very little pruning except in the spring when up to a third of the older wood at the base should be removed to promote new growth. If the whole plant is cut to the ground it will take several seasons to recover.*

Pruning out Problems

Apart from pruning a shrub to improve its shape, you may also need to prune out potential problems, such as damage and disease. Once a year, thoroughly check whether your plant needs attention.

CUTTING OUT DEAD WOOD

Cut out all dead wood from the shrub. This can be done at pruning time or at any other time of year when you can see dead material. Cut the dead wood out where it reaches live wood, which may be where the shoot joins a main stem or at the base of the plant. If the shrub is a large, tangled one, it may be necessary to cut out the dead branches bit by bit, as the short sections may be easier to remove than one long piece, especially if the stems have thorns that catch on everything.

CUTTING OUT CROSSING STEMS

Most shrubs grow out from a central point, with their branches arching gracefully outwards. However, sometimes a shoot will grow in towards the centre of the bush, crossing other stems in its search for light on the other side of the shrub. While there is nothing intrinsically wrong with this growth pattern, it is best to remove such branches as they will soon crowd the other branches and will often chafe against them, rubbing off the bark from the stem.

CUTTING OUT DIEBACK

I Tips of stems often die back, especially those that have carried bunches of flowers. Another cause is the young growth at the tip of shoots being killed by frost. If this die-back is not cut out, it can eventually kill off the whole shoot. Even if die-back proceeds no further it is still unsightly and the bush looks much tidier without these dead shoots. Cut the shoot back into good wood, just above a strong bud.

CUTTING OUT CROSSING STEMS

I Cut out the stems while they are still young and free from damage and disease. Using secateurs (pruners), cut the stem at its base where it joins the main branch.

CUTTING OUT DISEASED OR DAMAGED WOOD

I Cut any diseased or damaged wood back to sound wood, just above a strong bud. The wood is usually quite easy to spot. It may not be dead yet but still in the process of turning brown or black.

HARD PRUNING

1 There are a few shrubs — buddlejas are the main example — which benefit from being cut hard back each spring, much improving the foliage. Elders (*Sambucus*) and the purple smoke bush (*Cotinus*) are best treated in this way. *Rosa glauca* also responds very well to this type of pruning.

2 Cut the shoots right back almost to the ground, making the cuts just above an outward-facing bud and leaving little more than a stump. It may seem a little drastic, but the shrubs will quickly grow again in the spring. If they are not cut back, they become very leggy and do not make such attractive bushes.

3 Several plants that have attractive coloured bark in the winter are best cut to the ground in the spring.

4 So by the following winter, new attractive shoots will be displayed. The various coloured-stemmed *Rubus*, such as *R. cockburnianus* as well as some of the dogwoods (*Cornus* 'sibirica') and willows (*Salix*) are good candidates for this treatment.

DEAD-HEADING

1 Regular dead-heading will keep the shrub looking tidy and will also help promote further flowering. Roses, in particular, appreciate regular attention. Cut the flowering stems back to a bud or stem division.

Right: *The flowering on roses will always be improved if they are regularly dead-headed. This vigorous, multi-coloured rose is 'Miss Pam Ayres'.*

Weeding and Mulching

Strong, vigorous shrubs are able to grow in grass without much difficulty but, in most normal garden situations, a shrub border benefits visually and in health by being regularly weeded and protected with a suitable mulch.

WEEDING

Long grass growing through the lower branches of a bush makes it look untidy and is difficult to remove. Young shrubs, in particular, do not like competition from weeds. From the health point of view, weeds not only remove vital nutrients and moisture from the soil but, if the shrubs are small, weeds can smother them, preventing light from reaching the foliage. Another disadvantage of allowing weeds to grow under shrubs is that they provide a constant nuisance by seeding into the surrounding borders. If given regular attention, shrubs are not too difficult to weed.

Once they are established, the shade provided by the leaves tends to discourage weeds from germinating.

HAND WEEDING

Hand weeding is the best solution. A good start is provided by thorough soil preparation, when all perennial weeds are removed. If perennial weeds reappear under established bushes they can be very difficult to eradicate. Pull weeds out by hand, loosening them first with a fork. Avoid digging or hoeing too much around shrubs with shallow roots that are only just below the surface.

USING WEEDKILLER

Unless it is really necessary, it is best to avoid using chemical weedkillers around shrubs. It is so easy to damage or kill the shrub by mistake because most weedkillers will kill or damage whatever they come in contact with. Always follow the instructions on the packet carefully, and keep aside a special watering can to prevent harmful residues killing any of your other plants.

1 Treat deep-rooted weeds like ground elder and bindweed with a translocated weedkiller based on glyphosate, which is moved by the plant to all parts. Use a gel formulation to paint on where watering-in the weedkiller may damage plants nearby.

1 Removing weeds by hand is one of the surest ways of catching them all. Some people find this process tedious but, if carried out regularly, it need not be so. In fact, it is an opportunity to stop and examine the bushes at close quarters, not only to look for problems but to appreciate them. Use a small hand-fork to dig over the ground to leave a tidy finish.

2 Another method of removing weeds by hand is by hoeing. This is quick and simple, and best carried out in hot weather so that any weeds hoed up quickly die. A large hoe can be used but, for more control in confined areas, a small onion hoe is better.

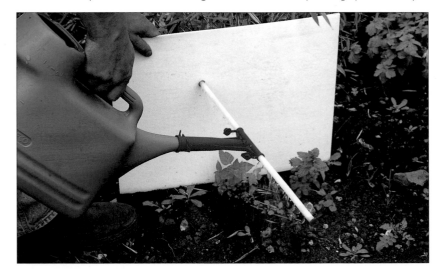

2 If it is possible to water on the weedkiller with a watering can, use a piece of board to shield those plants you don't want to be affected with the weedkiller. If the weeds are not deep-rooted, you could use a contact killer, although it is preferable to use a hoe to remove the weeds if possible.

MULCHING

Mulching has many benefits in the garden: the main one, from the gardener's point of view, is that it cuts down on the amount of time required for watering and weeding as it holds the moisture in and makes it difficult for weeds to get through. Never mulch over the top of perennial weeds and always ensure that the soil is moist before you mulch, watering the ground if needed. A wide range of mulches can be used. The most attractive are organic ones, but black plastic sheeting provides a good modern alternative, especially if it can be covered up with bark, gravel or compost. Always top up mulching, should it become thin and the earth or plastic begin to show.

USING MULCHES UNDER SHRUBS

1 Here, the potentilla is surrounded by bare earth. This provides an attractive finish as long as it is weed-free and dug over from time to time, to refresh the surface. But for a more labour-saving garden, it is best to add a mulch.

2 Grass clippings make a cheap and effective mulch. Never apply them too thickly – 5 cm (2 in) is the maximum depth, or the heat they produce as they decompose may harm the stems of the shrub. Never use mowings from grass that has gone to seed or the mulch could provide the reverse of its intended effect!

3 Chipped or composted bark is a very good mulch. It should be stored for several months to let it release any resin and start the decomposition. Some gardeners worry that it introduces fungal diseases, but the spores of these are already in the air and the bark does not appreciably increase the risk.

4 Plastic sheeting makes a very effective, if unattractive, mulch. Use plastic especially designed for garden use, which allows rain water to permeate through into the ground. If you lay the plastic before you plant the shrubs, cut holes in it and plant through it. On the other hand, if the shrub bushes are already in position, cut the plastic and tuck it in under the shrubs.

5 It is worth covering plastic with some other material. Gravel or small stones are ideal for this. Pour the gravel on to the plastic, making certain that there are no ridges or wrinkles in it that will poke up through the stones.

Above: *Gravel makes an ideal background against which to see the plants. It is easy to maintain and can be raked to keep its fresh appearance. Make certain that the plastic does not show through, as this can spoil the effect.*

Watering and Feeding

In the main, shrubs are easy to look after. Under normal conditions they do not need watering and, if their leaves are allowed to remain on the ground under and around the bushes, they do not need feeding. However, nature is capricious and there are times when the weather is extremely dry and watering is necessary. Some shrubs show stress much more readily than others. Hydrangeas, for example, are some of the first shrubs whose leaves hang limply when there is a shortage of moisture. They can be used as an indicator that conditions are worsening and it will soon be time for general watering.

WATERING SHRUBS

Selected areas of the garden such as small beds are best watered by hand with a watering can or hand-held spray. Larger areas can be dealt with by use of a sprinkler. Before watering, check to see if there are any restrictions on the type you can undertake: in drought years or areas of low rainfall, there may well be bans on sprinklers or the use of any method that involves hosepipes (garden hoses).

Whatever method you choose, watering is best carried out in the early morning or evening, before or after the sun gets its strength. The reason for this is that drops of water on the leaves and flowers can act as magnifying lenses, causing the sun to burn small brown spots on the foliage or petals. Although this may not actually be harmful to the plant, it can make it look diseased and is not very attractive.

1 When watering by hand, have patience and give the ground around the plant a thorough soaking. If in doubt, dig a small hole and check the water has soaked right down to the roots. Sinking tubes around a shrub and pouring water down these is a good way of ensuring the water reaches the right place.

2 A sprinkler has the advantage that you can turn it on and then get on with something else. Place a jam jar or a similar container under the spray, to gauge roughly how much has fallen. There should be at least 2.5 cm (1 in) of water in the jar for the sprinkler to have done any good.

WATERING ERICACEOUS PLANTS

Ericaceous plants such as rhododendrons and heathers should not be watered with water containing chalk or lime. When watering this type of plant, use rain water that has been collected in water butts or tanks. Other ericaceous plants include *Andromeda*, *Calluna* (heathers), *Camellia*, *Cassiope*, *Enkianthus*, *Gaultheria*, *Kalmia*, *Phyllodoce*, *Pieris* and *Vaccinium*.

1 If you bury a pipeline just beneath the ground you can plug in various watering devices. A sprinkler can simply be pushed on to this fitting which lies flush to the turf.

3 Drip-feed systems can be used for beds, borders and containers. "T" joints allow tubes to be attached for individual drip heads.

AUTOMATIC WATERING

In areas where there is a constant need to water, a permanent irrigation system employing drip-feed pipes may be well worth considering. Alternatively, you can use a watering system with a timing device, which will save you time and is also beneficial to the plants. There are many systems to choose from, so visit your local garden centre and look at advertisements to find out what is best for your needs.

2 Control systems can be fitted to the hose system so that you can alter the pressure of the water. These can also act as a filter.

4 The delivery tube of the hosepipe (garden hose) can be held in position with a pipe peg, if necessary.

FEEDING SHRUBS

If you mulch regularly, you probably won't need to feed any further. A light sprinkling of an organic, slow-release fertilizer, such as bonemeal, may be all that is required. However, when there is regular watering, such as to a shrub in a container, the soil can become drained of its nutrients and you will need to replace them. This can be done by adding a dry mixture by hand or by adding a liquid feed. Roses, in particular, benefit from an annual feed, which should be applied in spring or early summer after the dormant season of winter is over. Whenever possible, choose a slow-release or controlled-release fertilizer which will feed the plant throughout the summer.

SOLUBLE FERTILIZERS

1 Water-soluble fertilizer should be sprinkled around the edges of the shrub rather than near the stem, as most of the active root growth will be a distance from where the main stem is.

2 Gently hoe the fertilizer into the soil to help it penetrate the roots more quickly.

3 Water in thoroughly, particularly if the ground is very dry.

LIQUID FERTILIZERS

1 An alternative method of feeding is to use a liquid feed. This is most useful for shrubs in containers. Add the fertilizer to one of the waterings; in the case of container shrubs, this could be once every three weeks, but it would not be required so frequently in the open soil – once every three months or as recommended by the manufacturer.

Above: *Regular watering and feeding helps to keep plants at their best as the healthy foliage of this* Spiraea japonica *'Goldflame' shows.*

Dealing with Weather Problems

Weather, in particular winter weather, can cause problems for the shrub gardener. Throughout the year, winds can break branches of shrubs and, if there is any danger of this, shrubs should be firmly staked. If boughs or stems do break, cut them neatly back to a convenient point. If the wind is a constant problem, it becomes necessary to create a windbreak of some sort or shrubs will become permanently bent and, frequently, damaged.

PROTECTING AGAINST THE ELEMENTS

Frost can cause a lot of damage to shrubs, especially late or early frosts, which can catch new growth and flowers unexpectedly. General cold during the winter can be dealt with more easily, because it is relatively predictable: either cover the plants or plant them next to a wall, which will provide warmth and shelter.

Drought can be a problem, especially if it is not expected. Defend against drought when preparing the bed by incorporating plenty of moisture-retaining organic material. Once planted, shrubs benefit from a thick mulch, which will help hold the moisture in.

There are some plants that do not tolerate wet weather. Most plants with silver leaves, such as *Convolvulus cneorum* and lavenders prefer to grow in fairly dry conditions. Unfortunately there is little that can be done to protect such shrubs from the rain, although making their soil more free-draining by adding grit to the soil, or by growing them in well-drained containers usually helps.

Some shrubs prefer a shady position away from the sun. Many rhododendrons and azaleas, for example, prefer to be out of the hot sun. These can either be planted in the shade of a building or under trees or beneath taller shrubs.

WINDBREAKS

If there are perpetual problems with wind, it is essential to create some sort of windbreak. In the short term this can be plastic netting, but a more permanent solution is to create a living windbreak. A number of trees and shrubs can be used for this: *Leylandii* are often used, because they are one of the quickest-growing, but they are really best avoided for more suitable alternatives. They are thirsty and hungry plants that take a lot of the nutrients from the soil for some distance around their roots. They also continue growing rapidly past their required height.

It is best to get the windbreak established before the shrubs are planted but, if time is of the essence, plant them at the same time, shielding both from the winds with windbreak netting.

SHRUBS AND TREES FOR WINDBREAKS

Acer pseudoplatanus (sycamore)
Berberis darwinii
Buxus sempervirens (box)
Carpinus betulus (hornbeam)
Choisya ternata
Corylus avellana (hazel)
Cotoneaster simonsii
Crataegus monogyma (hawthorn)
Elaeagnus x ebbingei
Escallonia 'Langleyensis'
Euonymus japonicus 'Macrophyllus'
Fraxinus excelsior (ash)
Griselinia littoralis
Hippophaë rhamnoides (sea buckthorn)
Ilex (holly)
Ligustrum ovalifolium (privet)
Lonicera nitida (box-leaf honeysuckle)
Picea sitchensis (sitka spruce)
Pinus sylvestris (Scots pine)
Pittosporum tenuifolium
Prunus laurocerasus (cherry laurel)
Prunus lusitanica (Portuguese laurel)
Pyracantha (firethorn)
Rosmarinus officinalis (rosemary)
Sorbus aucuparia (rowan)
Tamarix (tamarisk)
Taxus baccata (yew)
Viburnum tinus (laurustinus)

Above: *Hedges are frequently used as windbreaks to protect the whole or specific parts of the garden. Whilst they are becoming established, they themselves may also need some protection, usually in the form of plastic netting. Here privet (*Ligustrum*) has been chosen.*

PROTECTING FROM WINTER COLD

1 Many shrubs, like this bay (*Laurus nobilis*) need some degree of winter protection. This shrub is in a container, but the same principles can be applied to free-standing shrubs. Insert a number of canes around the edge of the plant, taking care not to damage the roots.

2 Cut a piece of fleece, hessian (burlap) or bubble polythene (plastic) to the necessary size, making sure you allow for an overlap over the shrub and pot. Fleece can be bought as a sleeve, which is particularly handy for enveloping shrubs.

3 Wrap the protective cover around the plant, allowing a generous overlap. For particularly tender plants, use a double layer.

4 Tie the protective cover around the pot, or lightly around the shrub if it is in the ground. Fleece can be tied at the top as moisture can penetrate through, but if using plastic, leave it open for ventilation and watering.

5 Protecting with hessian (burlap) or plastic shade netting should be enough for most shrubs, but if a plant should require extra protection, wrap it in straw and then hold this in place with hessian or shade netting.

Above: *Late frost can ruin the flowering of a bush. This azalea has been caught on the top by the frost, but the sides were sufficiently sheltered to be unaffected. A covering of fleece would have given it complete protection.*

Right: *Lilac (*Syringa*) can be affected by late frosts which nip out the flowering buds preventing displays such as this.*

Growing Shrubs From Seed

Growing any plant from seed is a satisfying exercise and growing shrubs seems doubly so. When you see a fully mature shrub, perhaps covered in flowers, and know that you grew it from a small seed, you will have a justifiable sense of achievement. It is not a difficult process, but it is one that requires a bit of patience; many shrubs take a number of years between sowing and growing to reach flowering size. However, if you sow a few different shrubs each year, you will soon have a constant stream of new plants maturing and the wait will not seem too long.

PROPAGATION

Seed can be obtained from seed merchants, friends or one of the many seed exchanges run by horticultural clubs. More exotic and rare seed can be bought from various seed-collecting expeditions that advertise their products in specialist gardening magazines.

Sow the seed as soon as you get it and put the pots out in an open, shady place where they experience whatever the weather throws at them. Keep them watered in dry weather, but do not cover them in cold weather, as the cold will often help override any dormancy that there might be in the seed, which would prevent it from germinating. Bear in mind that germination might take a couple of years, so be patient. Seed that is encased in berries needs to have the fleshy part removed before sowing it.

There is rarely any need to sow seed in large quantities and so it is all right to sow in pots rather than trays. A 9 cm (3½ in) pot is usually the right size, as this will produce up to twenty seedlings.

1 Fill the pot right up to the rim with compost (soil mix). Settle it by tapping it sharply on the bench or table. Very lightly press down and level the surface with the base of a similarly sized pot. Do not press too hard. The level of the compost should now be below the rim of the pot.

2 Shrub seed is, on the whole, quite large and can be sown individually. Space them out on the surface of the compost so that they are equidistant. Do not be tempted to overfill the pot. If you have a lot of seed, use two pots. Smaller seed can be scattered over the surface but, again, do not overcrowd and ensure that they are well spaced.

3 Cover the seed and compost with a layer of fine grit, which should be at least 1 cm (½ in) thick. This will make it much easier to water the pot evenly as well as making it easier to remove any weeds, moss or liverwort that may start to grow on the surface. It also provides a well drained area around the rot-prone neck of the emerging seedling.

4 Before you do anything else, label the pot. One pot of seed looks exactly like any other pot and they will soon get into a muddle if the pots are not labelled. Include the name of the plant and the date of sowing on the labels. The source of the seed can also be useful additional information. Some gardeners like to keep a "sowing book", in which they record complete details of sowing and what happens afterwards, such as germination time and survival rates.

5 Water the pot with a watering can with a fine rose. Place the pot in the open, but shielded from the sun. Do not let it dry out.

PRICKING OUT

Once the seedlings have germinated, it is important to keep them growing on. Water them regularly and pot them on as soon as possible. This is important, as the sowing compost (soil mix) is not very rich in nutrients and the seedlings will soon become starved. In addition, if the seedlings are left in the pot for any length of time they will become overcrowded and very drawn and spindly. Most shrubs are best pricked out into individual plant pots rather than seed trays.

Use a good potting compost (potting soil) and refer to the section below about soilless and soil-based composts before sowing both seed and seedlings.

SEED AND POTTING COMPOST

Seed and potting composts (growing mediums) are a matter of personal preference. Some gardeners prefer soil-based composts while others swear by soilless ones. Seed seems happy in either but different composts seem to suit different regimes.

Soilless composts can be over-watered and remain very soggy but, on the other hand, once dried out they can be difficult to re-wet.

Soil-based composts are more free-draining, dry out more quickly but can be easily rewatered. They are also quite heavy compared with the soilless varieties. Try some of each and then stick to the one that suits your style of gardening best.

PRICKING OUT SHRUB SEEDLINGS

1 Invert the pot and tap it on the bench or table, so that the contents come out in one lump. Gently ease away part of the soil-ball and separate the seedlings from it. Touch or hold the seedlings only by the leaves and not by the stem or roots.

2 Fill the bottom of the pot with a little compost (soil mix) and then hold the seedling by a leaf over the centre of the pot, resting your hand on the edge of the pot to steady it. With the other hand, gently fill the pot with compost.

3 Gently tap the pot on the table to settle the compost, and lightly firm it down with the fingers, levelling off the surface. Add a 1 cm (½ in) layer of fine grit to the surface. Label the pot immediately.

4 Water the seedlings, either from below in a water bath or from above with a watering can with a fine rose. Place the pots in a shady spot, preferably under a closed cold frame for a few days and then slowly open the lights to harden the plants off.

Taking Cuttings

Raising new plants from seed is easy but takes rather a long time. The length of time between propagation and having a plant ready to go outside can be reduced by taking cuttings instead. Important as this may be, the real advantage of taking cuttings is that the resulting offspring are identical to their parent. Plants from seed, on the other hand, vary, sometimes so minutely that you cannot tell them apart but sometimes by a large amount: the leaves may be a different colour or the flowers a different size. Sometimes the variation is a welcome one and you obtain a new plant that is worth having, but, on the whole, the opposite seems to be the case. With cuttings, however, you always know what you are going to get.

SEMI-RIPE AND HARDWOOD CUTTINGS

Taking cuttings is a simple procedure. A heated propagator helps but it is not essential; you can use a simple plastic bag as a cover, to create an enclosed environment. Hardy plants will root outside, but they will need a cold frame to protect them.

There are two basic types of cuttings: semi-ripe and hardwood. The semi-ripe cuttings are taken from the current year's wood. They are taken from midsummer onwards at a point when the soft tips of the shoots are beginning to harden and are no longer quite as flexible. They are often just changing colour from a light green to a darker one.

Hardwood cuttings are taken from the shrubs at the shoot's next stage, when it has become hard, ready to experience the frosts of winter. These are taken from autumn onwards.

In both cases, always choose healthy shoots that are free of disease or damage. Avoid any that are covered with insect pests. Aphids, for example, transmit viral diseases as well as weakening stems. Avoid shoots which have become drawn and spindly by growing towards the light and have a long distance between leaves. Usually, the shoots near the top of the bush are better than those towards the base, where they are starved of light. Put all cuttings in a plastic bag as soon as you take them, to stop them drying out.

The compost (soil mix) to use is a cutting compost, which can be readily purchased. However, it is easy to make your own as it consists of 50 per cent (by volume) sharp sand and 50 per cent peat or peat substitute. Instead of sand, you can use vermiculite.

The cuttings are ready to be potted on once they have rooted. Usually new growth starts on the stem, but if not carefully dig up the root ball and check for new roots.

TAKING SEMI-RIPE SHRUB CUTTINGS

1 Choose a stem that is not too flexible and is just turning woody where it joins last year's hard growth. Cut it just above a bud and put the whole stem into a plastic bag. Collect several stems.

2 Cut the stem below a bud and make the top cut just above a leaf 10 cm (4 in) above the base leaf. Cleanly remove the bottom leaves with a sharp knife, leaving only the top leaves.

3 Dip the base of the stem into a rooting powder or liquid. This will help the cutting to root and also protect it, as the powder or liquid contains a fungicide. Tap the stem to remove the excess.

4 Make a trench in the compost (soil mix) with a small object and place the cutting in, making sure the base is in contact with the compost.

5 Firm the compost around the stem, so that there are no air pockets. Continue planting the other cuttings, making sure they are well spaced.

6 Water the compost and spray the leaves with a copper fungicide. Label the plant. If using a pot, place it in a propagator or cover with a plastic bag. If outside, place under a cold frame.

TAKING HARDWOOD CUTTINGS

In many ways, hardwood cuttings are even easier to take than semi-ripe ones, but they will take longer to root.

Once you have planted the cuttings, leave them in the ground until at least the next autumn, by which time they should have rooted. They will often produce leaves in the spring but this is not necessarily a sign that they have rooted.

Once you think they have rooted, test by digging one up. If they have, they can be transferred to pots or a nursery bed where they can be grown on to form larger plants before being moved to a permanent position.

1 Cut about 30 cm (12 in) of straight, fully ripened (hard) stem from a shrub.

2 Trim the stem off just below a leaf joint and remove any soft tip, so that the eventual length is about 23 cm (9 in) long. Remove any leaves.

3 Although a rooting hormone is not essential, it should increase the success rate, especially with plants that are difficult to root. Moisten the bases of the cuttings in water.

4 Choose a sheltered, shady spot in the garden and dig a slit in the ground with a spade. If the soil is heavy dig out a narrow trench and fill it with either cutting compost or sharp sand.

5 Insert the cuttings in the ground, leaving the top 7 cm (3 in) or so of the stem above ground.

6 Firm the soil around the cuttings to eliminate pockets of air that would cause the cuttings to dry out. Once the cuttings have rooted, dig them up and pot them on in the normal way. This will normally be the following autumn.

SHRUBS TO TRY

These are just some shrubs that will root from hardwood cuttings:

Aucuba japonica (spotted laurel)
Buddleja (butterfly bush)
Cornus (dogwood)
Forsythia
Ligustrum
Philadelphus (mock orange)
Ribes (currant)
Rosa
Salix (willow)
Sambucus (elder)
Spiraea
Viburnum (deciduous species)

Layering

Layering is a good way of producing the odd few extra plants without a propagator. It is a useful method of producing one or two plants from a bush that somebody might want, without all the bother of what might be termed "formal" propagation. It is not a difficult technique and, after the initial work, nothing has to be done until the new plant is ready for transplanting – and it does not require any special equipment.

FOLLOWING NATURE

Basically, layering is simply persuading the plant to do what it often does in the wild (and in the garden, for that matter) and that is to put down roots where a branch or stem touches the ground. Encourage this by burying the stem and holding it in position with a peg or stone, so that the wind does not move it and sever any roots that are forming. It is as simple as that. Frequently, you will find that nature has already done it for you and a search around the base of many shrubs will reveal one or more layers that have already rooted on their own.

While layering might sound a casual way of propagating, it is a good one to try if you have difficulty in rooting cuttings. Being connected to the parent plant, the shoot still has a supply of nutrients and is, therefore, still very much alive, whereas a cutting may well have used up all its reserves and died before it has had a chance to put down roots. A layer is also far less prone to being killed off by a fungal disease.

DIVISION

Shrubs suitable for division produce multiple stems from below the ground or increase by suckering or running (self-layering). At any time between autumn and early spring, dig up one of the suckers or a portion of the shrub, severing it from the parent plant with secateurs (pruners) or a sharp knife and replant or pot up the divided portion. Suitable shrubs include *Arctostaphylos*, *Calluna*, *Clerodendrum bungei*, *Cornus alba*, *C. canadensis*, *Erica*, *Gaultheria*, *Holodiscolor*, *Kerria*, *Leucothoe*, *Mahonia*, *Nandina*, *Pachysandra*, *Rubus*, *Sarcococca* and *Sorbus reducta*.

1 Choose a stem that will reach the ground without breaking and prepare the ground beneath it. In most cases, the native soil will be satisfactory but if it is heavy clay add some potting compost (potting soil) to improve its texture.

2 Trim off any side-shoots or leaves. Dig a shallow hole and bend the shoot down into it.

3 To help hold the shoot in place, peg it down with a piece of bent wire.

4 Fill in the hole and cover it with a stone. In many cases, the stone will be sufficient to hold the layer in place and a peg will not be required. The stone will also help to keep the area beneath it moist.

5 It may take several months, or even years, for shrubs that are hard to propagate to layer but, eventually, new shoots will appear and the layer will have rooted. Sever it from its parent and pot it up into a container.

IMPROVING ROOTING

Although it is not essential, rooting can be improved with difficult subjects by making a slit in the underside of the stem at a point where it will be below ground. This slit can be propped open with a thin sliver of wood or a piece of grit. This cut interrupts the passage of hormones along the stem and they accumulate there, helping to promote more rapid rooting.

If several plants are required, it is quite feasible to make several layers on the same shoot, allowing the stem to come above the surface between each layer. This is known as "serpentine layering".

Above: *Rhododendrons frequently self-layer in the wild and may also do so in the garden, but the prudent gardener always deliberately makes a few layers just in case a visiting friend takes a liking to one of the varieties that he grows.*

6 If the roots are well developed, transfer the layer directly to its new site.

DESIGNING A BORDER

Drawing a Border Plan

There are several ways of designing a border. The majority of gardeners undoubtedly go for the hit-and-miss approach, simply putting in plants as they acquire them. Then, if they feel inclined, they may move them around a bit to improve the scheme. Many good gardens have been created in this way but a more methodical approach tends to produce better results from the outset. However, do not be fooled: no method produces the best results first time. Gardening is always about adjustment, moving plants here and there to create a better picture or to change the emphasis or mood.

MAKING A SKETCH

The most methodical approach to designing a border is to draw up a plan and to work from this. Making a plan is one of the many enjoyable parts of gardening. It involves choosing the plants that you want to grow, sorting them into some form of pattern and committing this to paper, so that you can follow it through. A further refinement is to produce a drawing of what the border will roughly look like at different stages of the year. You do not have to be an artist to do this; it is for your own satisfaction and, since no one else need see it, the drawing can be quite crude!

The plan itself should, preferably, be drawn up on squared paper (graph). This will help considerably in plotting the size and relationship of plants. The sketches can be on any type of paper, including the back of an envelope, if you can't find anything else at the time.

Decide whether you are going to treat the garden as a whole or whether you are going to concentrate on a single border. This border will need to be accurately measured if it is already in existence or you must firmly decide on its intended shape and dimensions.

Draw up a list of the plants that you want to grow, jotting details alongside as to their colour, flowering period, eventual height and spread and their shape.

Plot the plants on the plan, making sure you show them in their final spread, not the size they are in their pots. Bear in mind details such as relative heights, foliage and flower colour. These can be further explored by making an elevation sketch of the border as seen from the front. It can be fun to colour this in with pencils or watercolours, to show roughly what it will look like in the different seasons.

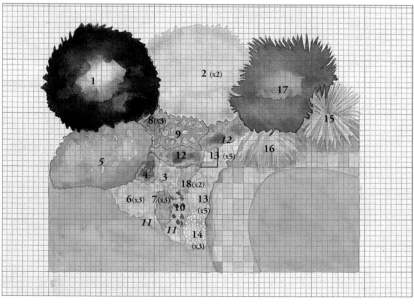

Key

1. *Cotinus coggyria* 'Royal Purple'
2. *Weigela florida* 'Florida Variegata'
3. *Perovskia atriplicifolia* 'Blue Spire'
4. *Allium chrisophii*
5. *Daphne x burkwoodii* 'Somerset'
6. *Sedum spectabile* 'September Glow'

7. *Eryngium giganteum*
8. *Digitalis purpurea*
9. *Rosa* 'Wenlock Castle'
10. *Papaver somniferum*
11. *Astrantia major*
12. *Salvia forsskaolii*

13. *Stachys byzantina*
14. *Lychnis coronaria* 'Alba'
15. *Yucca gloriosa* 'Variegata'
16. *Phormium cookianum*
17. *Berberis thunbergii* 'Rose Glow'
18. *Dictamnus albus purpureus*

Above: *It will take a few years before your plans and sketches develop into the established border you would like to see.*

Designing with Shrubs

Of all aspects of gardening, designing a garden or border is probably one of the most exciting and, at the same time, one of the most difficult. It requires the ability to see things that are not yet there and to assemble whole groups of different plants in the mind's eye.

THE BASIC ELEMENTS

Most people have an awareness of the basic elements of garden design from other disciplines; most of us, for example, are adept at choosing what clothes to wear. We know what colours go together and what suits our shape and height. We are aware that certain fabrics add a touch of luxury to an outfit and that certain colours create a bright effect, while others produce a more subtle image. Similarly, most people are at least involved in decorating their home, where again the choice of colours, textures and finishes have become almost second nature over the years.

PERSONAL TASTE

The same principles we apply to choosing clothes and items for the home are used when designing in the garden, with many of the choices coming from an innate feeling for what the gardener likes and dislikes. This means that, like clothing, gardens are personal, with the fortunate result that each garden is different from the next. By all means be inspired by ideas seen in other gardens, but do not slavishly imitate another garden: the chances are that it will not work in your situation – the climate might be slightly different or the soil might be wrong. There are no definite rules with regards to design; there is no ultimate garden. However, there are a few guidelines that the experience of many centuries of gardening have produced, and it is worth bearing these in mind.

THE SHAPE OF THE BORDER

A border can be any shape, to suit the garden. Curved edges tend to create a more informal, relaxed feeling, while straight edges are more formal. The one point to remember is that the border should not be too narrow. Shrubs look better in a border where they have room to spread without being too crowded. A border that is only wide enough to take one shrub at a time has a habit of looking more like a hedge than a border. A wider border also allows the gardener to build up a structure of planting, which is more visually satisfying.

Left: *An attractive border filled with a mixture of shrubs and herbaceous plants designed to provide interest over a long period of time. Shrubs in flower include the blue* Ceanothus, *white* Olearia, *purple* Lavandula stoechas *and the white* Prostanthera cuneata, *with a purple rhododendron in the background.*

PART OF THE SCHEME

Shrubs need not be confined to borders – they can become part of the overall scheme of the garden. This is particularly important where the garden is small and there is little room for formal borders. Shrubs can be mixed with other plants or simply used in isolation, as focal points that draw the eye. They can be taken out of the ground and used in pots or other containers, or grown against walls and fences. Besides being part of the design, they can have a sense of purpose, perhaps to screen a dustbin (trash can) or to create a perfumed area near where people sit in the evening.

HEIGHT AND SHAPE

Shrubs have a lot to offer the designer as there is such a wide choice of attributes that can be applied to them. Shrubs come in all sorts of shapes and sizes, from tiny dwarf ones to those that are difficult to distinguish from trees. The general principle of design is to put the tallest at the back and smallest at the front. This must not be rigidly adhered to or the the border will begin to look like choir stalls, all regularly tiered. Bring a few of the taller ones forward and place some of the shorter ones in gaps between bigger ones. This makes the border much more interesting and prevents the viewer from taking in the whole border at a glance.

The different shapes of the plants also add variety. Some are tall and thin, others short and spreading. The latter are particularly useful as ground cover and can be woven in and out of other shrubs as if they were "poured" there. Heathers are especially useful for this.

Above: In this small garden, shrubs are not only used to make an interesting background of different textures, shapes and colours, but are also planted in containers to break up the foreground. To complete the picture, formal hedges hold the whole scheme together.

Right: This attractive border builds up beautifully from the front but, at the same time, is not regimented as the heights vary along its length. It demonstrates well the effectiveness of differently-shaped shrubs and other plants while, at the same time, illustrating the importance of colour and leaf shapes.

Using Colour in the Border

Colour is an extremely important aspect of shrub gardening, perhaps more so than other areas because shrubs not only offer a large range of flower colours but also a vast range of foliage colour and texture.

MIXING COLOURS

Colour is the most tricky thing to get right in the garden. It is essential to spend time looking at other gardens and looking at pictures in books and magazines, to see how colours are best handled. It is not just a question of saying that reds mix well with purples: some do, others do not. Orange-reds and blue-reds are quite different from each other and cannot all be used in the same way.

A good garden will combine all the colours in a variety of ways in all areas. Sticking to just one style, especially in a large garden, can become boring. In a small garden, trying to mix too many different colour schemes has the reverse effect and may become uncomfortable.

Using shrubs gives colour in both leaves and flowers. When planning, it is important that the foliage of the various plants blends well together as they are generally around for a long time – all year, in fact, if they are evergreen. Try not to use too many different colours of foliage together and avoid too many variegated shrubs in one place as this can look too "busy". The colour of nearby flowering plants can also enhance the foliage.

Colours can also be affected by the texture of the leaves. A shiny green leaf can light up a dull area almost as brilliantly as a gold leaf while a soft, hairy foliage adds a sense of luxury.

Right: *The sharp contrast between the silver leaves of the* Elaeagnus *'Quicksilver' and the purple of the flowers of* Erysimum *'Bowles Mauve' makes a beautiful, if startling, combination.*

Below: *Here, the purple flowers of* Lavandula stoechas pedunculata *make a much softer contrast to the purple-leaved sage* Salvia officinalis *'Purpurascens'.*

Left: The bright red stems of Cornus alba *'Sibirica' add a great deal of interest to the winter scene, especially if sited so that the low sun strikes them.*

Right: A dwarf willow, Salix repens, *grows with the ground-hugging* Lithodora diffusa. *The contrast in the flowers makes this an exciting combination in the spring and, for the rest of the year, the different foliage shapes make them an interesting ground cover.*

COLOURFUL STEMS

It is not only the leaves and flowers of shrubs that have colour: stems, too, can provide it. This is particularly true in the winter, when the leaves are off most shrubs and there is little to lighten the grey scene. White, yellow, green, red and black stems then come into their own. Plants grown for their winter stems are often uninteresting for the rest of the year and so should be planted where they will not be noticed in summer but will stand out in winter.

Right: It is possible to jazz up the appearance of the garden with bright colour combinations, such as this azalea and alyssum, Aurinia saxatilis. *The dazzling picture they create is wonderful but, fortunately, neither plant lasts in flower too long, otherwise the effect would become tiresome.*

Mixing Shrubs

Shrub borders or shrubberies have died out as gardens have become smaller. In many ways, the border devoted to only shrubs would be a labour-saving form of gardening, but being able to mix in a few other plants helps to make it more interesting.

GROWING SHRUBS WITH PERENNIALS AND ANNUALS

As well as being more interesting from a visual point of view, mixing shrubs and other plants creates a greater variety of different habitats in the garden for a greater range of plants. For example, there are many herbaceous plants, many coming from wooded or hedgerow habitats in the wild, that need a shady position in which to grow. Where better than under shrubs? Many of these, such as the wood anemone, *Anemone nemorosa*, appear, flower and die back in early spring before the leaves appear on the shrubs, thus taking up a space that would be unavailable later in the season once the foliage has obscured the ground beneath the shrub.

Herbaceous plants can also be used to enliven a scene where all the shrubs have already finished flowering. For example, if you have a number of rhododendrons, most will have finished flowering by early summer and will be comparatively plain for the rest of the year. Plant a few herbaceous plants between them and retain interest for the rest of the year.

Herbaceous plants also extend the range of design possibilities. For example, it might not be possible to find a shrub of the right height that blooms at the right time with the right-coloured flowers. One of the thousands of hardy perennials may offer the perfect solution. Similarly, the combination of textures and shapes might not be available in shrubs, so look to see if there are herbaceous or annual plants that will help solve the problem.

In the early stages of the establishment of a shrub border or a mixed border, the shrubs are not likely to fill their allotted space. To make the border look attractive in the meantime, plant annuals or perennials in the gaps. These can be removed as the shrubs expand. As well as improving the appearance of the border, the plants will also act as a living mulch and help to keep weeds at bay.

WOODLAND PLANTS FOR GROWING UNDER SHRUBS

Anemone nemorosa (wood anemone)
Brunnera macrophylla
Campanula latifolia
Convallaria majalis (lily-of-the-valley)
Cyclamen hederifolium
Eranthis hyemalis
Euphorbia amygdaloides robbiae (wood spurge)
Galanthus (snowdrop)
Geranium
Helleborus (Christmas rose)
Polygonatum
Primula

Above: *This* Lychnis chalcedonica *adds the final touch to a good combination of foliage. Without it, the grouping might seem dull compared with other parts of the garden in the summer.*

Above: *The geranium in the foreground is the right height and colour to match the roses and the ceanothus behind. It would be hard to find a shrub to fit in with this combination.*

Left: *Sometimes, one startling combination acts as a focal point and draws the eye straight to it. This combination of the blue flowers of a ceanothus and the silver bark of the eucalyptus is extraordinarily beautiful. There are many such combinations that the gardener can seek and this is one of the things that makes gardening so satisfying and even, at times, exhilarating.*

Above: *A good combination of textures, shapes and colours is achieved here with the cardoon (*Cynara cardunculus*) providing interesting colour and structure, while the* Salvia sclarea *in the front provides the subtle flower colour.*

CHOOSING SHRUBS

Hedges

Few gardens are without a hedge of some sort. They are used as a defensive barrier around the garden as well as having a more decorative purpose within. The defensive role is to maintain privacy both from intruders and prying eyes (and, increasingly, against noise pollution). This type of hedge is thick and impenetrable, often armed with thorns to discourage animals and humans pushing through. Hedges also have less sinister functions, more directly related to gardening. One is the important role of acting as a windbreak to help protect plants. Another is to act as a foil for what is planted in front of it. Yew hedges, for example, act as a perfect backdrop to herbaceous and other types of border.

Above: *A formal beech hedge (*Fagus sylvatica*) makes a neat and tidy boundary to any garden. Beech, yew (*Taxus baccata*) and hornbeam (*Carpinus betulus*) also make good formal hedges as long as they are kept neat. They are all slow growing and need less attention than many others.*

USING HEDGES

Hedges are widely used within the garden, where they are perhaps better described as screens or frames. Screens are used to divide up the garden, hiding one area from view until you enter it. In some cases, the hedges are kept so low that they can hardly be called hedges; they are more like decorative edging to a border. Box reigns supreme for this kind of hedge. Others are informal hedges, in which the plants are allowed to grow in a less restricted way, unclipped, so they are able to flower, adding to their attraction. Roses and lavender are two popular plants for using like this.

We all want hedges that grow up as quickly as possible and usually end up buying one of the fastest growers. However, bear in mind that once grown to the intended height, these fast growers do not stop, they just keep growing at the same pace. This means that they need constant clipping to keep them under control. A slower growing hedge may take longer to mature, but once it does, its stately pace means that it needs far less attention. In spite of its slow-growing reputation, in properly prepared ground, yew will produce a good hedge, 1.5–2 m (5–6 ft) high in about 5 to 6 years from planting.

Right: *Although often much maligned, leyland cypress (*x Cupressocyparis leylandii*) makes a good hedge. The secret is to keep it under control and to clip it regularly. Here, although soon due a trim, it still looks attractive, as the new growth makes a swirling movement across the face of the hedge.*

Above: *This tapestry hedge is made up of alternate stripes of blue and gold conifers. Here, the bands have been kept distinct but, if deciduous shrubs are used, the edges often blend together, which gives a softer appearance.*

Above: A *country hedge makes an attractive screen around the garden. This one is a mixture of shrubs, all or most of them being native trees: there is box (*Buxus sempervirens*), hawthorn (*Crataegus monogyna*), hazel (*Corylus avellana*) and holly (*Ilex aquifolium*). The only problem with this type of hedge is that the growth rates are all different so it can become ragged looking, but then country hedges always are!*

Left: *An informal flowering hedge is formed by this firethorn (*Pyracantha*). The flowers make it an attractive feature while the powerful thorns give it a practical value as an impenetrable barrier. Flowering hedges should not be clipped as frequently as more formal varieties and trimming should be left until flowering is over.*

Above: *Informal hedges of lavender border a narrow path. The joy of such hedges is not only the sight of them but the fact that, as you brush along them, they give off the most delicious scent. Such hedges fit into a wide variety of different situations within a garden.*

Maintaining a Hedge

Planting a hedge in most respects is like planting any shrub. Prepare the ground thoroughly as the hedge is likely to stay in place for many years, possibly centuries.

INGREDIENTS FOR A HEALTHY HEDGE

Add plenty of organic material to the soil, both for feeding the hedge and for moisture retention. If the ground lies wet, either add drainage material or put in drains. Plant the hedge between autumn and early spring. For a thick hedge plant the shrubs in two parallel rows, staggering the plants in each. Water as soon as it is planted and keep the ground covered in mulch. Use a netting windbreak to protect the hedge if it is in an exposed position.

CLIPPING HEDGES

If a hedge is neglected, it soon loses a lot of its beauty. Regular trimming soon helps to restore this but it is also necessary for other reasons. If the hedge is left for too long, it may be difficult to bring it back to its original condition. Most can be restored eventually but this can take several years. A garden can be smartened up simply by cutting its hedges. Untrimmed hedges look ragged and untidy. Some types of hedging material need more frequent trimming than others, to keep them looking neat.

1 Cutting a hedge also includes clearing up the trimmings afterwards. One way of coping with this task is to lay down a cloth or plastic sheet under the area you are clipping and to move it along as you go.

2 When using shears, try to keep the blades flat against the plane of the hedge as this will give an even cut. If you jab the shears forward with a stabbing motion, the result is likely to be uneven.

WHEN TO CLIP HEDGES

Buxus (box)	late spring and late summer
Carpinus betulus (hornbeam)	mid/late summer
Chamaecyparis lawsoniana (Lawson's cypress)	late spring and late summer
Crataegus (hawthorn)	early summer and early autumn
x Cupressocyparis leylandii (leyland cypress)	late spring, midsummer or late spring, early autumn
Fagus sylvatica (beech)	mid/late summer
Ilex (holly)	late summer
Lavandula (lavender)	spring or early autumn
Ligustrum (privet)	late spring, midsummer and early autumn
Lonicera nitida (box-leaf honeysuckle)	late spring, midsummer and early autumn
Prunus laurocerasus (laurel)	mid-spring and late summer
Prunus lusitanica (Portuguese laurel)	mid-spring and late summer
Thuja plicata (thuja)	late spring and early autumn
Taxus (yew)	mid/late summer

3 A formal hedge looks best if it is given a regular cut. The top, in particular, should be completely flat. This can be best achieved by using poles at the ends or intervals along the hedges, with strings tautly stretched between them. These can be used as a guide. Take care not to cut the strings! If you have room to store it, make a template out of cardboard in the desired shape of the hedge so that the shape of the hedge is the same each time you cut it.

4 Keep the blades flat when you cut the top of a hedge. If it is a tall hedge, you will need to use steps rather than trying to reach up at an angle.

5 Power trimmers are much faster than hand shears and, in consequence, things can go wrong faster as well, so concentrate on what you are doing and have a rest if your arms feel tired. Wear adequate protective gear and take the appropriate precautions if you are using an electrically operated tool. Petrol- (gasolene-) driven clippers are more versatile, in that you are not limited by the length of the cord or by the charge of the battery, but they are much heavier than the electrically-powered equivalent.

6 Some conifers are relatively slow growing and only produce a few stray stems that can be cut off with secateurs (pruners) to neaten them. Secateurs should also be used for large-leaved shrubs, such as laurel (*Prunus laurocerasus*). This avoids leaves being cut in half by mechanical or hand shears, which always looks a bit of a mess.

Above: *A well-shaped hedge should be wider at the bottom than it is at the top. This allows the lower leaves to receive plenty of light and thus prevents the bottom branches from drying out.*

Ground Cover

One of the most valuable uses of shrubs is as ground cover. Ground cover is what its name implies, planting that covers the ground so that no bare earth shows. While there are obvious visual attractions in doing this, the main benefit is that ground cover prevents new weeds from germinating and therefore reduces the amount of maintenance required.

PLANTS FOR COVER

In the main, ground-covering plants are low-growing, but there is no reason why they should not be quite large as long as they do the job. Large rhododendron bushes form a perfect ground cover, for example, as nothing can grow under them.

Some ground-covering plants have flowers to enhance their appearance – heather (*Erica* and *Calluna*) and *Hypericum calycinum*, for example – while others depend on their attractive foliage – ivy (*Hedera*) and euonymus are examples.

Ground cover will not stop established weeds from coming through; it does inhibit the introduction of new weeds by creating a shade that is too dense for the seed to germinate and that starves any seedlings that do manage to appear.

SHRUBS SUITABLE FOR PLANTING AS GROUND COVER

Acaena
Arctostaphylos uva-ursi
Berberis
Calluna vulgaris (heather)
Cistus (rock rose)
Cotoneaster
Erica (heather)
Euonymus fortunei
Hebe pinguifolia 'Pagei'
Hedera (ivy)
Hypericum calycinum
Juniperus communis 'Prostrata'
Juniperus sabina tamariscifolia
Juniperus squamata 'Blue Carpet'
Lithodora diffusa
Pachysandra terminalis
Potentilla fruticosa
Salix repens
Stephandra incisa
Vinca minor (periwinkle)

Above: *A solid block of gold shimmers above the soil. The evergreen* Euonymus fortunei *'Emerald 'n' Gold' makes a perfect ground cover plant because it is colourful and dense.*

Right: *Prostrate conifers perform well. One plant can cover a large area and the texture and colour of the foliage makes it a welcome feature. They have the advantage of being evergreen and thus provide good cover all year round.*

Above: *The periwinkles, especially* Vinca minor, *make good ground cover. They are evergreen and will thrive in quite dense shade. However, if you want them to flower well it is better that they are planted more in the open.*

Above: *In the rock garden, the ground-hugging* Salix repens *rapidly covers a lot of territory. It can be a bit of a thug and needs to be cut back from time to time, to prevent it from spreading too far.*

Above: Lithodora diffusa *is one of those plants that straddles the divide between hardy perennials and shrubs, because it is classed as a subshrub. It provides a very dense ground cover for the rock garden and, in the early spring, makes a wonderful carpet of blue.*

Right: *By late summer and into autumn, much ground cover is looking a bit tired and jaded. However,* Ceratostigma plumbaginoides *is still flowering and presents a good choice of plant for providing colour at this time of year.*

Planting Ground Cover

The benefits of ground cover only occur if the ground has been thoroughly prepared. Any perennial weeds left in the soil when the shrubs are planted will soon come up through the cover as it will not control existing weeds, it will only prevent new ones germinating.

TENDING GROUND COVER

Once planted, the space between the shrubs should be constantly tended until the plants have grown together, and from then on they truly create ground cover. Take care when planning ground cover as it is not something you want to replant too often.

Although one of the aims of using ground cover is to reduce maintenance by cutting out weeding, it still requires some attention and may need trimming once a year. Ivy, for example, looks much better if it is sheared in the late winter or early spring and hypericum should be cut back after flowering.

1 It is important to remove any weeds from the soil where you are going to grow ground cover, otherwise the weeds will grow through the shrubs which will make them very difficult to eradicate.

2 Thoroughly prepare the soil in the same way as you would for any other type of shrub. Dig in plenty of well rotted organic material.

3 Position the plants in their pots so that you get the best possible layout, estimating how far each plant will spread. The aim is to cover all the bare earth eventually.

4 Dig holes and plant the shrubs. Firm them in so that there are no air pockets around the plants and then water the shrubs well.

5 The gaps between the plants may take a year or more to close up. In the meantime, plant annuals, perennials or other shrubs to act as temporary ground cover while the main plants spread. Arrange the "fillers" in their pots first, so you can create the most effective planting.

Right: *When you are satisfied with the arrangement you have, plant the fillers and water them in. Remove them when the main ground cover takes over.*

GROUND COVER PLANTS FOR SHADY AREAS
Acuba
Cassiope
Cornus canadensis (dogwood)
Euonymus
Gaultheria
Hedera (ivy)
Lonicera pileata
Pachysandra
Rhododendron
Sarcococca
Vaccinium
Vinca minor (periwinkle)

MAINTAINING GROUND COVER

1 Ground cover is often neglected and, because it is a low, permanent planting, it tends to collect all kinds of litter and rubbish. Take time to regularly clean through all your ground cover, removing any litter that is lurking between the leaves.

2 Most ground cover benefits from being trimmed back at least once a year. Here, the periwinkle *Vinca minor* is given a much-needed trim.

3 Regular trimming means that the ground cover grows at a more even rate, with fewer straggly stems. It looks tidier and healthier.

Dwarf Shrubs

In the small garden and the rock garden, dwarf shrubs are much more in keeping with the scale of things than large plants. Being small, they also have the advantage that you can grow more varieties in the same space.

USING DWARF SHRUBS
Size apart, dwarf shrubs are no different from the larger ones and are treated in exactly the same way. They can be used by themselves in rock gardens or separate beds. Or they can be mixed in with taller shrubs, perhaps in front of them or even under them. Many dwarf shrubs make very good ground cover plants. They can also be used in pots and other containers, either in groups or as specimen plants.

ROCK GARDEN SHRUBS
The really small dwarf shrubs are usually grown in the rock garden and even in troughs. Many are not much more than a few centimetres high. Like their larger brethren, they are equally grown for their foliage and flowers. Some are perfect miniatures of larger plants. *Juniperus communis* 'Compressa', for example, could be a large conifer seen through the reverse end of a telescope.

Above: *For those who like bright colours, nothing could fit the bill better than* Genista lydia. *In spring, it is absolutely covered with a mound of bright, gold-coloured, pea-like flowers. It looks good tumbling over rocks or a wall but can be used anywhere. It requires very little attention.*

Above: *Most ceanothus are large shrubs, often needing wall protection to bring them through the winter. C. 'Pin Cushion' is a miniature version for the rock garden. It still retains both the good foliage and the blue flowers that attract so many gardeners to this group of plants and has the advantage that it needs little attention.*

Above: *As well as the more common dwarf shrubs, there are many varieties that will appeal to those who may want to start a collection of unusual shrubs:* x Halimiocistus revolii *is one example. This beautiful plant spreads to form a mat of dark green leaves, dotted with white flowers in midsummer. It likes a well-drained soil but needs little attention.*

Above: *The rock rose (Helianthemum) is one of the great joys of dwarf shrubs. There are many different varieties, with a wide range of colours, some bright while others are more subtle. The colour of their foliage also varies, from silver to bright green. Rock roses are suitable for the rock garden, raised beds or mixed borders. They spread to make large sheets, but rarely get tall. They need to be sheared over after flowering, to prevent them from becoming too sprawling.*

Above: *There are a number of dwarf willows of which this,* Salix helvetica, *is one of the best. It forms a compact shrub with very good silver foliage. It can be used in a rock garden or wherever dwarf shrubs are required. It looks especially good with geraniums –* G. sanguineum, *for example – growing through it. This willow needs very little attention.*

Left: *The group of dwarf conifers growing in this rock garden is* Juniperus communis *'Compressa'. This is one of the very best varieties of dwarf conifer, because it never grows very high, usually not more than 45 cm (18 in), and it takes many years to reach that height. Their slow growth rate means they are useful for alpine troughs and they have the advantage that they need very little attention.*

Above: *Using a few dwarf shrubs and conifers in a trough or sink adds to the height of the planting, giving it more structure and interest than if it were simply filled with low-growing alpine plants.*

Planting a Gravel Bed

Most dwarf rock garden plants need a well-drained soil with plenty of grit or sharp sand added to it. Plant between autumn and spring, as long as it is not too wet or cold. They look best grown with other alpine plants, set amongst rocks or in gravel beds. The miniature landscape of the trough can be designed in the same way.

DWARF SHRUBS FOR THE ROCK GARDEN

Aethionema	*Hypericum* (many dwarf
Berberis (dwarf forms)	forms)
Ceanothus prostratus	*Juniperus communis*
Chamaecyparis obtusa	'Compressa'
(and various 'Nana' forms)	*Leptospermum scoparium*
Convolvulus cneorum	'Nanum'
Convolvulus sabatius	*Lithodora diffusa*
Daphne	*Lonicera pyrenaica*
Dryas octopetala	*Micromeria corsica*
Erica (heather)	*Ononis*
Euonymus nana	*Salix helvetica*
Euryops acreus	*Salix repens* (and several
Fuchsia procumbens	other forms)
Genista lydia	*Sorbus reducta*
x *Halimiocistus revolii*	*Teucrium* (various dwarf forms)
Hebe (many dwarf forms)	*Thymus* (many forms)
Helianthemum (most forms)	*Verbascum* 'Letitia'

1 Prepare the ground for planting. Dig the ground to allow about 5 cm (2 in) of gravel. Level the ground and lay heavy-duty black plastic or a mulching sheet over the area, overlapping strips by about 5 cm (2 in).

2 Tip the gravel on top of the plastic and level it off with a rake.

3 Draw the gravel back from the planting area and make a slit in the plastic. Plant in the normal way.

4 Firm in the plants and pull back the plastic, then cover again with gravel.

Right: *A rock garden with dwarf and slow-growing shrubs.*

WOODLAND BEDS

As well as a rock garden built in the sun, with free-draining material, many rock gardeners also have what is traditionally known as a woodland or peat bed, although other materials besides peat are now used for planting. The beds are positioned in part shade, where they catch dappled sunlight or sun only at the end of the day. Here, in a woodland-type soil, a wide range of plants that like damp, shady conditions can be grown. Amongst these are many dwarf shrubs, perhaps the most popular being the dwarf rhododendrons.

The soil here is usually a mixture of leaf mould and good garden soil. In the past, quantities of peat were also used, although a peat substitute, such as coir, is now commonly used instead. The soil is usually acidic in nature, suiting many of the plants that grow in woodland conditions. The peat, or peat substitute, gives it the right pH balance, although it is possible to make soil more acid by adding rotted pine needles to it.

DWARF SHRUBS FOR A WOODLAND BED
Andromeda
Arctostaphylos
Cassiope
Daphne
Erica (heather)
Gaultheria
Kalmia
Kalmiopsis
Pernyetta
Phyllodoce
Rhododendron (many dwarf forms)
Vaccinium

Above: *Daphnes are excellent dwarf shrubs to use in the garden. They all have deliciously scented flowers and many, such as this* D. tangutica, *are evergreen. They have the advantage that they very rarely need any pruning, just the removal of dead wood should any occur. They can be used in rock gardens or elsewhere.*

Top right: *Heathers make good all-year-round plants and appreciate the acid nature of a woodland bed.*

Right: *A colourful woodland bed can be made up of heathers and conifers. This kind of bed is low maintenance, although the heathers stay tighter and more compact if they are sheared over once a year.*

Evergreens

The great feature of evergreens is the fact that they hold on to their leaves throughout the winter. They can be used as a permanent part of the structure of any border or garden. This has advantages and disadvantages. The advantage is that throughout the year there is always something in leaf to look at; on the other hand, unless carefully sited, evergreens can become a bit dull, so plan your planting with care.

WORK-FREE GARDENING

In many respects, evergreen shrubs form the backbone of a work-free garden, because they need very little attention unless they are used as hedging, where they need regular clipping. Although they do not drop their leaves in autumn, as deciduous bushes do, they still nonetheless shed leaves. This is usually done continuously through the year.

Many evergreens have dark green leaves, which can make the scene in which they are used a bit sombre but this effect can be brightened with the use of plants with variegated leaves. Because evergreen leaves have to last a long time, many are tough and leathery, with a shiny surface. This shine also helps to brighten up dull spots, reflecting the light back towards the viewer.

Evergreens are no more difficult to grow than other shrubs; indeed they are easier because they need less maintenance.

Above: *Conifers can become boring and so familiar that you do not even see them. However, there are some that provide a wonderful selection of shapes and textures. This juniper produces an attractive "sea of waves" effect that can never become boring.*

Left: *Privet is a good evergreen shrub although in its common form it is better known as a hedging plant. This is* Ligustrum lucidum *'Excelsum Superbum'. In the open the variegation is golden but in shade it becomes a yellowish green.*

Left: *Choisya is a good evergreen. The leaves are shiny and catch the sun and it produces masses of white flowers in spring and often again later in the year. These perfume the air for a good distance around. This form with golden foliage is* C. ternata *'Sundance'.*

Above: *One tends to think of evergreens as being dull green and without flowers, but there are many that put on a magnificent display of flowers each year. Rhododendrons are a good example of this.*

Below: *This* Pieris japonica *is an evergreen that will grace any garden, as long as the area is not prone to late frosts. The foliage alters its colour as it matures, providing a constantly changing picture. This is enhanced by long plumes of white flowers.*

Above: *Many of the hebes are evergreen. This one, H. cupressoides, belongs to the whipcord group; it has very small leaves pressed tightly against its stems and, when out of flower, it could easily be mistaken for a conifer.*

Shrubs with Coloured Foliage

Most foliage is green, but the discerning gardener will soon notice that the number of different greens is almost infinite. A lot can be done by careful arrangement of these various greens, but even more can be achieved by incorporating into the garden the large number of shrubs that have foliage in other colours besides green.

VARYING SHADES OF GREEN

Leaves need green chlorophyll to function, so leaves are never completely devoid of green, another colour may just dominate. For example, yellow foliage still has a green tinge to it and purple likewise. Scrape back the hairs that make a leaf look silver or grey and, again, there will be green. When grown out of the sun, particularly later in the season, this green becomes more apparent. Occasionally, stems bearing paper-white leaves appear on some shrubs. It would be wonderful if one could propagate these by taking cuttings but, unfortunately, their total lack of chlorophyll means they will not grow.

MAINTAINING THE COLOUR

Purple leaves need the sun to retain their colour. Silver-leaved plants must always be grown in the sun; they will not survive for long in shade. Golden and yellow foliage often need a dappled shade – too much sun and the leaves are scorched. However, too much shade and the leaves turn greener, so the balance is a delicate one. The thing to avoid is midday sun.

Growing coloured-leaved shrubs is no different from any other shrub. They need the same pruning, except that if a reversion occurs, this must be cut out.

As well as shrubs with single-coloured foliage, there are shrubs with foliage in two or more colours, known as "variegated" foliage, and shrubs which are planted for their autumn foliage – just two other interesting aspects of the coloration of shrubs.

> ### SILVER FOLIAGE
>
> *Caryopteris x clandonensis*
> *Convolvulus cneorum*
> *Elaeagnus* 'Quicksilver'
> *Hebe pinguifolia* 'Pagei'
> *Hippophaë rhamnoides*
> *Lavandula angustifolia*
> *Pyrus salicifolia* 'Pendula'
> *Rosa glauca*
> *Salix lanata*
> *Santolina chamaecyparis*
> *Santolina pinnata neapolitana*

BETTER FOLIAGE

Coppicing or pollarding some coloured-leaved shrubs improves the quality of the leaves. It produces bigger and often richer-coloured foliage. Cut the plants back in the early spring, before growth begins. They will quickly regain their original size but the foliage will be bigger and better. *Sambucus* (elder), *Cotinus* (smoke tree) and *Rosa glauca* all benefit from this.

Above: Rosa glauca *has the most wonderful glaucous (grey- or blue-green) foliage with a purple-blue tint which contrasts well with the pink and white flowers. The foliage is improved by coppicing.*

POLLARDING

1 Cut back the stems to very short stubs, leaving perhaps one or two buds on each stem to grow. The treatment looks a bit drastic, but a mass of new shoots will be produced during the summer, with colourful stems in winter.

2 A head of brightly-coloured branches will stem from the base in the winter as on this *Salix alba vitellina* 'Britzensis'.

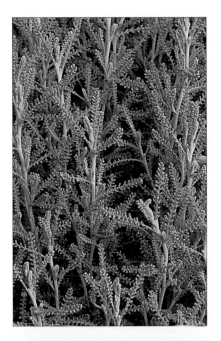

Left: *Silver foliage is very desirable. All silver plants need a sunny position and a well drained soil, this cotton lavender,* Santolina chamaecyparis *being no exception. Shear the plant over in the spring, just as new growth begins, to keep it compact. Many gardeners also prefer to cut off the flowering stems, because they find the sharp yellow flowers too harsh.*

Below: *This shrub grows in areas that are too dry to grow many other plants. It has had many names over the years and is now called* Brachyglottis *(Dunedin Group)* 'Sunshine'.

Above: *The silver leaves of plants can often set off the colour of their flowers beautifully. Here, the silvery-grey leaves of* Helianthemum 'Wisley Pink' *are a perfect foil for its pink flowers. Shear over the plant after flowering, to keep it from becoming straggly.*

Above: *A favourite silver-leaved shrub is* Elaeagnus 'Quicksilver' *which in the sunshine looks like burnished pewter. During the spring, the leaves are supplemented by masses of small, pale primrose-yellow flowers which as well as being attractive have a delicious scent that wafts all over the garden.*

Shrubs with Purple Foliage

Purple foliage is a very useful component when designing a garden. It forms a pleasant alternative to the normal green, without being quite as stark in contrast as silver, yellow or one of the variegated foliages.

A Pleasant Contrast

Purple is ideal as a main background colour or in combination with other plants as it goes with most other colours. It works well, in particular, as a background to various coloured flowers, so can be used with herbaceous or annual plants.

The one big drawback with purple foliage is that it can look very heavy and leaden if used in too great a quantity. A few shrubs will work better than too many. But purple can look superb if placed where the evening sunlight comes from behind the shrub so that the leaves are backlit. They then positively glow with colour and no other shrub can match them.

PURPLE-LEAVED SHRUBS

Acer palmatum
  'Atropurpureum'
Berberis thunbergii
  'Atropurpurea'
Berberis thunbergii
  'Bagatelle'
Cordyline australis
  'Atropurpurea'
Corylus maxima 'Purpurea'
Cotinus coggygria 'Royal
  Purple'
Fagus sylvatica 'Riversii'
Prunus cerasifera 'Nigra'
Salvia officinalis
  'Purpurascens'
Weigela florida 'Foliis
  Purpurea'

Above: *A really rich purple is to be seen on* Prunus x cistena. *This is beautifully enhanced in the spring by numerous pink flowers with purple centres. The total effect can be stunning.*

Left: *This* Cercis canadensis *'Forest Pansy' has purple foliage, exquisitely flushed with green and greenish blue. The heart-shaped leaves add to the attraction of this bush. In the autumn, the leaves take on a bright scarlet hue.*

Left: *The hazels (Corylus) have several purple forms to offer. They generally have large, imposing leaves. However, if they are in too shady a place they are liable to turn green.*

Right: *Another very good series of purples are the various smoke bushes,* Cotinus. *They look especially effective when they are planted so that the evening sun shines through the leaves. Cutting this shrub back hard in the spring produces much larger leaves the following year.*

Above: *In some shrubs, the colour is in the young leaves and once they begin to mature, they revert to their original colour. Although in some ways this is disappointing, in others, as here with this purple sage, the effect can be stunning.*

Above: *A good source of purple foliage is* Berberis thunbergii 'Atropurpurea' *in its various forms, including a dwarf one. In the autumn, the leaves colour-up beautifully and the shrub has the added attraction of red berries.*

Shrubs with Variegated Foliage

There has been a steady increase of interest in variegated shrubs and today they can be seen in one form or another in most gardens. This increase of interest is most welcome, because it has stimulated the search for more types of variegated plants and now there are many more from which to choose.

TYPES OF VARIEGATION

There are many different types of variegation. First there is the aspect of colour. Most variegations in shrubs are gold, followed very closely by cream and white. These have the effect of lightening any group of plants they are planted with. They are particularly useful in shade or in a dark corner, because they shine out, creating interest where it is often difficult to do so. Other colours include different shades of green. Again, these have a lightening effect. On the other hand, variegation that involves purples often introduces a more sombre mood. Sometimes, there are more than two colours in a variegation and this leads to a sense of gaiety, even if combined with sombre colours.

When looked at closely there are several different patterns of variegation. From a distance the differences blur and the leaves just register as variegated, but if you get closer you can see how the variegation can alter the appearance of the leaves. In some cases, it is the edges of the leaves that are variegated, sometimes as a ribbon and in others as an irregular margin, perhaps penetrating almost to the centre of the leaves. Another common type is where the centre of the leaves are variegated. Sometimes this is an irregular patch in the centre and in others the variegation follows the veins of the leaf. Yet a third form of variegation is where the leaves are splashed with an alternative colour, as though paint has been flicked onto their surface. A final type is where the variegation appears as long parallel strips down the leaves.

All these are attractive and it is worth looking out for and collecting at least one of each type. The more one looks at this group of plants, the more fascinating they become.

SILVER AND WHITE VARIEGATION

Cornus alternifolia 'Argentea'
Cornus alba 'Elegantissima'
Cornus controversa 'Variegata'
Euonymus fortunei 'Emerald Gaiety'
Euonymus fortunei 'Silver Queen'
Euonymus fortunei 'Variegatus'
Euonymus japonicus 'Macrophyllus Albus'
Fuchsia magellanica 'Variegata'
Prunus lusitanica 'Variegata'
Rhamnus alaternus 'Argenteovariegata'
Vinca minor 'Argenteovariegata'

Above: *The variegated* Weigela florida *'Albomarginata' is seen here against a spiraea. The white-striped leaves blend well with the white flowers of the spiraea in spring, and in summer the interest is continued because the weigela produces pink flowers.*

Below: Cornus mas *'Aureoelegantissima' creates a very different effect here, by being planted next to a different type of plant. Here the colours are more muted and do not provide such a contrast as they do against the leaves of the* Geranium x oxonianum.

Above: *One of the most popular of variegated plants,* Cornus mas *'Aureoelegantissima', is shown here with* Geranium x oxonianum *growing through it. This is an easy plant to grow and its subtle coloration means it can grow in a wide variety of situations.*

Left: Rhamnus alaternus *'Argenteovariegata', as its name implies, has a silver variegation. This is present as stripes down the margins of the leaves and sets the whole shrub shimmering. It can grow into quite a large shrub, up to 3.5–4.5 m (12–15 ft) high.*

CUTTING OUT REVERSION IN SHRUBS

Variegation is an abnormality that comes about in a number of different ways. Frequently, the process is reversed and the variegated leaves revert to their original green form. These green-leaved stems are more vigorous than the variegated ones, because they contain more chlorophyll for photosynthesis and thus produce more food. If these vigorous shoots are left, they will soon dominate the shrub and it may eventually all revert to green. The way to prevent this is to cut out the shoots as soon as they are seen.

Above: *Green-leaved shoots have appeared in this* Spiraea japonica *'Goldflame'. If left, they may take over the whole plant. The remedy is simple. Remove the affected shoots back to that part of the stem or shoot where the reversion begins.*

Shrubs with Variegated Foliage 2

USING VARIEGATED PLANTS

Variegated plants should be used with discretion. They can become too "busy": if several are planted together they tend to clash. Reserve them to use as accent plants, to draw the eye. Also use them to leaven a scene, brightening it up a bit.

On the whole, variegated shrubs are no different in terms of planting and subsequent maintenance to any other plants, although you may need to consider how much sunlight they can tolerate.

Although many variegated shrubs will tolerate full sun, many others prefer to be away from the hot midday sun, in a light, dappled shade. Always check the planting instructions when you buy a new shrub, to see what situation it requires.

Above: *Several of the herbs, such as thyme, rosemary and sage, can be variegated. Here, the sage* Salvia officinalis *is shown in the yellow and green form 'Icterina'. As well as providing a visual attraction throughout the year, these evergreen variegated forms of herbs are also always available for use in the kitchen.*

Above: *This elder,* Sambucus racemosa 'Plumosa Aurea', *is not, strictly speaking, a variegated plant, but the variation from the young brown growth to the golden mature leaves gives the overall impression of a variegated shrub. In order to keep this effect, prune the elder almost to the ground each spring.*

YELLOW AND GOLD VARIATIONS

Abutilon metapotamicum
  'Variegatum'
Aucuba japonica 'Picturata'
Aucuba japonica 'Mr Goldstrike'
Aucuba japonica 'Crotonifolia'
Caryopteris x clandonensis
  'Worcester Gold'
Cornus alba 'Spaethii'
Daphne x burkwoodii
  'Somerset Gold Edge'
Euonymus fortunei 'Sunshine'
Euonymus fortunei 'Gold Spot'
Euonymus japonicus
  'Aureopictus'
Ilex aquifolium 'Golden
  Milkboy' (centre)
Ilex aquifolium 'Aurifodina'
  (edge/centre)
Ilex x altaclerensis 'Golden
  King' (edge)
Ilex aquifolium 'Crispa
  Aureopicta' (centre)
Ilex x altaclerensis
  'Lawsoniana' (centre)
Ligustrum ovalifolium 'Aureum'
Osmanthus heterophyllus
  'Goshiki'
Sambucus nigra
  'Aureomarginata'

Above: *There are many variegated evergreens that can add a great deal of interest to what could otherwise be a collection of plain, dark green shrubs. The hollies, in particular, provide a good selection. This one is* Ilex x altaclerensis *'Lawsoniana'. Its green berries have yet to change to their winter colour of red.*

Above right: Berberis thunbergii *'Rose Glow' is a beautifully variegated shrub, its purple leaves splashed with pink. It is eye-catching and fits in well with purple schemes. Avoid using it with yellows.*

Right: *An exotic variegation is seen on this* Abutilon megapotamicum *'Variegatum', with its green leaves splashed with gold. It has the added attraction of red and yellow flowers that appear in the latter half of the summer and continue into the autumn. It is on the tender side and in colder areas should be grown in pots and moved inside for the winter.*

Shrubs with Fragrant Foliage

There are a surprising number of shrubs with fragrant foliage. Some fragrances might not be immediately apparent, because they need some stimulant to produce it. Rosemary, for example, does not fill the air with its perfume until it is touched. Some of the rock roses (*Cistus*) produce a wonderfully aromatic scent after they have been washed with rain. Similarly, the sweet-briar rose (*Rosa rubiginosa*) and its hybrids, such as 'Lady Penzance', produce a delightfully fresh scent after rain.

WHERE TO PLANT

It is a good idea to plant shrubs with aromatic foliage near where you walk, so that when you brush against them they give out a delicious aroma. Few gardeners can resist running their fingers through rosemary foliage as they pass, and a lavender path is a pleasure to walk along, because the soothing smells of the herb are gently released along the path as you go.

For hot, dry gardens, *Camphorosma monspeliaca* is one of the best plants to grow, because it smells of camphor when the new shoots are touched. Thyme planted in the ground may be too low to touch with the hands, but it releases its fine fragrance if it is walked on in paving. Many conifers have a pleasant, resinous smell when they are rubbed. Juniper, in particular, is good.

But, of course, not all smells are pleasant. *Clerodendron bungei* has sweetly-scented flowers, but its leaves smell revolting if they are crushed. Many people dislike the sharp smell of the foliage of broom (*Cytisus*) and elder (*Sambucus*).

Above right: *While it is sensible to plant thyme used for the kitchen in a more hygienic position, it does make a wonderful herb for planting between paving stones because when crushed by the feet it produces a delicious fragrance – and trampling on it does not seem to harm the plant. Beware doing so in bare feet though, because there may well be bees on the thyme.*

Right: Prostanthera cuneata *is an evergreen shrub that has leaves with a curious aromatic scent that is very appealing. In spring, and again in the summer, white, scented flowers are produced, which look very attractive against the dark foliage.*

SHRUBS WITH FRAGRANT FOLIAGE

Aloysia triphylla
Laurus nobilis (bay)
Lavandula (lavender)
Myrica
Myrtus communis (myrtle)
Perovskia
Rosmarinus (rosemary)
Salvia officinalis (sage)
Santolina

Above: *One of the most beguiling of garden scents is that of rosemary, another culinary herb. If given a sunny well-drained site, this shrub will go on growing for many years, until its trunk is completely gnarled and ancient looking.*

Above: *Culinary herbs are a great source of scented foliage. Sage, for example, has a dry sort of herby smell, which will usually evoke in the passer-by thoughts of delicious stuffing mixtures. This is an evergreen and provides fragrance all year round.*

Right: Hebe cupressoides, *like so many plants, has a smell that is characteristically its own. It is a resinous type of fragrance that is reminiscent of the cypresses after which it is named.*

Shrubs with Fragrant Flowers

It is always worthwhile to include at least a few shrubs in the garden that have fragrant flowers. Unlike foliage scents, which generally need to be stimulated by touch, flower fragrances are usually produced unaided, and flowers will often fill the whole garden with their scent. This is particularly noticeable on a warm evening.

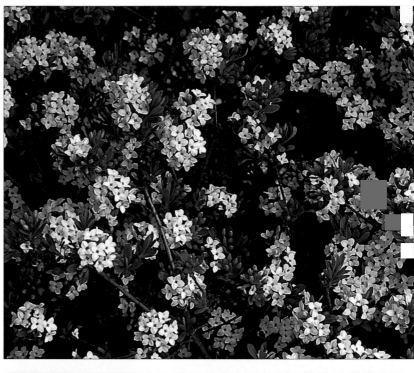

SOOTHING SCENTS

A good position for fragrant shrubs is next to a place where you sit and relax, especially after the day's work. The soft fragrance from the shrubs helps to soothe tiredness if put next to a seat or perhaps near an arbour or patio where you sit and eat. Psychologically, it can help to plant a shrub that has evening fragrance near the front gate or where you get out of the car, so that you are welcomed home by characteristically soothing scents. Choose an evening-scented shrub so that you do not get the scent on your way out in the morning, or you might not get to work at all! Another good position for a fragrant shrub is near a window or door that is often open, so the scents drift into the house.

As with foliage scents, some flowers smell unpleasant. Many dislike the smell of privet flowers, while the scent from *Cestrum parqui* is foetid in the day but sweet in the evening and at night.

One way to store summer fragrances is to turn some of the flowers into *potpourri*. Roses, in particular, are good for this.

In the winter, a surprising number of winter-flowering shrubs have very strong scents that attract insects from far away. Always try to include a few of these, such as the winter honeysuckles, in the garden.

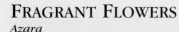

FRAGRANT FLOWERS

Azara
Berberis x stenophylla
Clethra
Corylopsis
Daphne
Elaeagnus
Hamamelis (witch hazel)
Itea
Magnolia
Mahonia
Myrtus (myrtle)
Osmanthus
Philadelphus (mock orange)
Rhododendron luteum
Sarcococca (sweet box)
Skimmia

Above right: *Daphnes are a good genus of plants for fragrance, because they nearly all have a very strong, sweet scent.* Daphne x burkwoodii *is one of the largest of the genus, seen here in its variety 'Somerset'. When in full flower in the spring, it will perfume a large area.*

Right: *The Mexican orange-blossom,* Choisya ternata, *is another sweet-smelling shrub. It flowers in the spring and then sporadically again through the summer. The delightful flowers contrast with the glossy foliage.*

Above: *Not everybody likes the smell of elder flowers, and even fewer people like the smell of elder leaves, but the flowers do have a musky scent that is popular with many country people.*

Left: *Many flowers produce a sweet scent in the spring and early summer and this* Viburnum x juddii *and its close relatives are always amongst the best examples. It produces domes of pale pink flowers with a delicious perfume that spreads over quite a wide area.*

Above: Philadelphus *(mock orange) is one of the most popular of fragrant shrubs. The combination of the pure white flowers (sometimes tinged purple in the centre) and the sweet perfume seems to remind many people of purity and innocence. They flower after many of the other sweet-smelling flowers are over.*

Above: *The most popular perfumed shrub of all must surely be the rose. One of the advantages of many modern varieties of rose is that they continue to flower and produce their scent over a long period, often all the summer and well into the autumn. 'Zéphirine Drouhin' has a wonderful scent and is repeat-flowering. It can be grown either as a bush or as a climber and has the added advantage of being thornless.*

Shrubs with Berries and Fruit

It is not just the leaves and flowers that make a shrub worth growing. Flowering usually produces some form of seed, which is often carried in an attractive casing of fruit or berry. Two of the oldest fruiting shrubs to be appreciated, even back in ancient times, are the holly and the mistletoe.

THE APPEAL OF FRUIT

Fruit, either as berries, seed pods or even fluffy heads, often enhances the appearance of a shrub, especially if the fruit is brightly-coloured. Fruit bushes, such as gooseberries and red currants, can be fan-trained or grown as standards, and many berried shrubs have been specially bred to increase the range of colours. The firethorn (*Pyracantha*) can now be found with red, orange or yellow berries, for example.

Berries and fruit are not only attractive to gardeners, but to birds and other animals, so if you want to keep the berries buy a shrub like skimmia which will not be eaten by them.

One thing to bear in mind with berrying shrubs is that the male and female flowers may be on separate plants (skimmias and hollies, for example). Although they will both flower, only the female with bear fruit. So if you want fruit or berries, make sure you buy a male and a female.

Left: *Pyracantha makes a very decorative display of berries in the autumn. There are several varieties to choose from, with the berry colour varying from yellow, through orange to red. The berries are not only attractive but good food for the birds.*

Below: *It is important when buying pernettyas (*Gaultheria mucronata*) that you buy both a male and a female plant to ensure that pollination takes place. One male will suffice for several females that carry the berries.*

BERRIED SHRUBS

Chaenomeles (japonica)
Cotoneaster
Crataegus (hawthorn)
Daphne
Euonymus europaeus
Hippophaë rhamnoides
Ilex (holly)
Ligustrum
Rosa
Symphoricarpo
Viburnum opulus

Right: Piptanthus *is not totally hardy and is normally grown against a wall for protection. After its yellow flowers in spring, it produces these attractive pods, which decorate the plant in midsummer.*

Left: *When buying holly, ensure that you buy a berry-bearing form as not all carry them. Seen here in flower is* Ilex aquifolium *'Ferox Argentea'.*

Right: *Skimmias are good plants for the winter garden as they have very large, glossy berries, with the advantage that the birds do not like them, so they remain for a long period. Ensure you get a berrying form and buy a male to pollinate them.*

Below: *The cotoneasters produce a brilliant display of berries, as well as having attractive leaves and flowers. The berries are not too popular with birds and are often left until all the other berries have been eaten.*

Above: *Rose heps or hips provide an extension to the rose's season. The colour varies from variety to variety, with some being red and others orange, and some, such as* R. pimpinellifolia, *bearing black berries.*

Shrubs for Containers

Such is the versatility of shrubs that they can be grown successfully in containers as well as in the open ground. Container shrubs can be positioned on hard surfaces such as patios, walls or on steps. They can also be grown in roof gardens, on balconies or in basement plots.

WHY CHOOSE CONTAINERS?

If the garden is small or paved, there is no reason why all the plants should not be grown in containers, particularly because they can be attractive in their own right. Any kind of shrub can be grown in a container, so long as the shrub is not too big or the container too small.

One advantage of growing shrubs in pots is that you can tailor the soil to the shrub's requirements. Probably the best thing about this is the fact that it is possible to grow acid-loving plants, such as rhododendrons and azaleas, in areas where the soil is naturally alkaline and where such plants would not normally grow. Camellias, pieris, gaultherias, vacciniums and heathers are among other such plants which need special soil.

Above: *A glazed ceramic container is used to house a combination of lavender and* Euonymous fortunei *'Emerald Gaiety'; as long as they do not outgrow their container, such combinations can create a most attractive picture.*

Right: *Most elders make a large shrub after a few years, but they can still be used as pot plants, especially if cut to the base each spring. Here* Sambucus racemosa *'Plumosa Aurea' is growing in a large substitute-stone container. It is used as part of a larger planting.*

Above: *It is often possible to plant shrubs that form large bushes in containers for a few years while they are still small and then replace them with the same or another plant. Here* Cornus mas *'Aureoelegantissima' which could eventually grow to 6 m (20 ft) or more is being used.*

Above: *Fuchsias make exceptionally attractive container plants. The more tender varieties need to be over-wintered inside or started again each year, but hardier varieties can be left outside in milder climates.*

Right: *Acid-loving shrubs like this rhododendron benefit from being grown in containers, where they can have the soil they need.*

SHRUBS FOR CONTAINERS

Ballota pseudodictamnus	*Ilex* (holly)
Buxus sempervirens (box)	*Indigofera*
Callistemon citrinus (bottlebrush)	*Kalmia*
Camellia	*Laurus nobilis* (bay)
Convolvulus cneorum	*Lavandula* (lavender)
Cordyline australis	*Myrtus communis* (myrtle)
Cotoneaster	*Olearia* (daisy bush)
Erica (heather)	*Phormium* (New Zealand flax)
Fuchsia	*Rhododendron*
Hebe	*Rosa*
Helianthemum	*Rosmarinus* (rosemary)
Hydrangea	*Skimmia*
Hypericum	*Yucca*

Planting Shrubs in Containers

There is no great difficulty in growing plants in containers, so long as you remember that the pots are likely to need watering every day, except when it rains, and possibly more often than this in the summer.

CONTAINER CARE

When planting shrubs in containers, it is essential to use a good potting compost (potting soil) that contains plenty of grit or sharp sand, to help with drainage, and to add small stones to the pot so that excess water can drain away. In addition, a slow-release fertilizer and some water-retaining granules will encourage the plant to flourish.

Bear in mind that your plant will not grow indefinitely if it is kept in the same pot or compost (soil mix) for ever. Every year or so, remove the shrub and repot it using fresh compost. If the shrub is becoming pot-bound, that is,

the roots are going round the edge of the container, forming a tight knot, either put it in a larger pot or trim back some of the offending roots.

POSITIONING CONTAINERS

If you have a large enough garden, it is possible to keep the containers out of sight and only bring them into view when the shrubs are at their best, in full flower, for example. In a smaller garden, where this is more difficult, move the pots around so that the best ones are always in the most prominent position and even hiding the others if this is possible.

1 All containers should have a drainage hole in the bottom. Loosely cover this and the bottom of the pot with broken pottery, bits of tile or small stones, so that any excess water can freely drain away.

2 Partially fill the container with compost (soil mix) and then mix in some water-retaining granules. These essential granules will swell up and hold many times their own weight in water to give up to the plant's roots when they want it. While not considerably reducing the amount of water needed, water-retaining granules will make it easier for the shrub to come through really hot and dry times in midsummer. Follow the instructions on the packet as to quantities you need for the size of the pot you have.

3 Place the container in the position you finally want to have it and continue filling it with compost (the pot will be heavy to move once it is fully-planted). Plant the shrub to the same level as it was in its original container. Firm the compost down lightly and top up, if necessary, with some further compost.

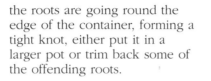

4 Most composts contain fertilizers but the constant watering will soon leach (wash) it out. A slow-release fertilizer can be mixed with the compost or a tablet, as here, can be added to the pot, which will give six months' supply of nutrients. Read the packet for any special instructions.

5 Leave the top of the compost as it is, or cover it with stones of some sort, such as large pebbles, as here, or gravel. These not only give the container an attractive finish but help keep the compost cool and prevent water from evaporating.

6 Finally, water the container thoroughly and continue to do so at regular intervals. During hot weather, this is likely to be at least daily.

7 You may want to keep the newly-planted pot out of sight until the shrub has matured or comes into flower. However, if the container is large, it is often best to fill it *in situ*, because it will be very heavy once filled with compost.

Right: *This variegated pieris, which likes an acid soil, would soon languish and die in a chalky garden.*

Shrubs for Topiary

Most shrubs are grown naturally. They may be cut back if they get too big, or trimmed if they are part of a hedge, but their natural shape is not generally altered. However, there is one class of shrub-growing in which the shape is drastically altered, so much so that it takes a close look to identify the plants involved. These are topiaries.

PRODUCING A SHAPE

Topiaries can be cut to any shape the gardener desires. They can be formed into abstract or geometrical shapes, such as balls, cones or pyramids, or they can be made into something more intricate, perhaps depicting a bird, a person or even a teapot. There is little limit to what the imagination can produce in topiary.

Tight, slow-growing shrubs are the ones to choose for topiary, with yew and box being the best. Holly (*Ilex*), privet (*Ligustrum*) and box-leaf honeysuckle (*Lonicera nitida*) are also recommended. Several others can also be used, but they need a lot more attention to keep them neat.

The simplest topiaries are "carved" out of solid shrubs, particularly if they are yew or box, because these will easily regenerate and slowly fill out to their new shape. However, the most satisfactory way to produce topiary is to train the shrubs to their shape from the very beginning. A metal or wooden former or template helps with this. The shoots are tied in and trimmed as they grow, until the shrub has acquired the desired shape. Some formers are just a rough guide to the shape, intended to hold the main pieces in position, especially if they are

vulnerable, such as a peacock's tail, but others are shaped like the finished work and can be used as a trimming guide when the work is complete.

Topiaries can take several years to reach completion, so do not get too impatient. Several projects can be started in pots at the same time, so there is always something going on to keep the interest alive.

TOOLS FOR TOPIARY

Unless the topiary is on a large scale, avoid using powered tools. It is too easy to lose concentration or momentary control and disaster follows. In preference, use hand tools, which take longer but which give you more control. For cutting thicker stems, especially in the initial training, use secateurs (pruners), snipping out one stem at a time. Once the shape has been formed, trim it over with normal hedging shears or a pair of clippers of the type usually used for sheep-shearing. The latter give excellent control, but can only be used for light trimming, such as removing the tips of new growth. If the topiary is made from a shrub with large leaves, then use secateurs to trim it to avoid cutting the leaves in half, otherwise they will die back with a brown edge and the overall appearance will be spoiled.

Above: *In this topiary a four-masted ship in full sail glides across the garden. Here, the complicated design is slightly obscured by other topiaries in the background.*

Above: *This practical piece of topiary has a wooden seat worked into the bottom of the shrub, supported on a metal frame. A complete set round a table would be a novel feature for a barbecue or outdoor meal.*

Above: *These simple shapes worked in box can be used to advantage in a wide variety of positions in the garden. They will take several years of dedication to produce, but the effort is definitely worth it.*

Above: *Gardens do not have always to be serious: there is a sense of fun about this jolly witch, sitting around her cauldron with her cat and its mouse, which would cheer up anybody looking at it.*

Above: *Topiary shapes can be as precise or as free as you wish. In this free interpretation of a simple windmill, cut from yew, you can sense the pleasure of the person who created it.*

Shrubs in Spring

Shrubs come into their own in the spring. This is the time when everything is waking up and looking fresh and the gardener's own enthusiasm is at its greatest.

SPRING FLOWERS

Many shrubs flower in spring, which gives them ample time to produce seed and for it to ripen and be distributed to ensure the next generation.

The one big enemy of spring-flowering shrubs is the severe late frosts that occur in some areas. A false start to the spring brings warm weather and then a sudden frost kills all the new shoots and knocks off the flower buds. Rhododendrons, azaleas, pieris, magnolias and many others frequently suffer this fate. One solution is to give some protection if hard frost is forecast. Placing a sheet of fleece over them is often sufficient.

It is tempting to put all the spring shrubs together, for one glorious display, but resist this or, at least, mix in a few later-flowering ones as well or the area could become dull for the rest of the year. One solution is to plant *viticella* clematis through them. These are cut back to the ground in late winter so that they do not interfere with the shrubs' flowering, but grow up and cover them in blooms from midsummer onwards.

Try and finish planting any new shrubs by early spring and, as the various shrubs finish flowering, prune them as necessary. Remember to feed those that are in containers.

Above: *Camellias flower from the late winter through to the middle of spring. They are best planted where they do not get the early-morning sun, as this will destroy the buds if they have been frosted overnight.*

Right: *One of the earliest shrubs to flower is* Spiraea *'Arguta' which produces a frothy mountain of pure white flowers over quite a long period. Sometimes it will even produce a few blooms in midwinter, to brighten the gloom.*

Above: *The flowering currant,* Ribes sanguineum, *is a beautiful spring-flowering shrub, but its foliage has a distinctive 'foxy' smell that not everyone likes.*

Above: Exochorda x macrantha *'The Bride' is a showy, spring-flowering plant. When in full flower, it is so covered in pure white flowers that the leaves are barely visible. Here, many of the flowers are still in bud, forming attractive ribbons of white balls.*

Above: *Rhododendrons are many gardeners' favourite spring shrub. They need an acid soil and a position out of hot sunlight. They can be bought in a wide variety of colours, some soft and subtle and others bright and brash.*

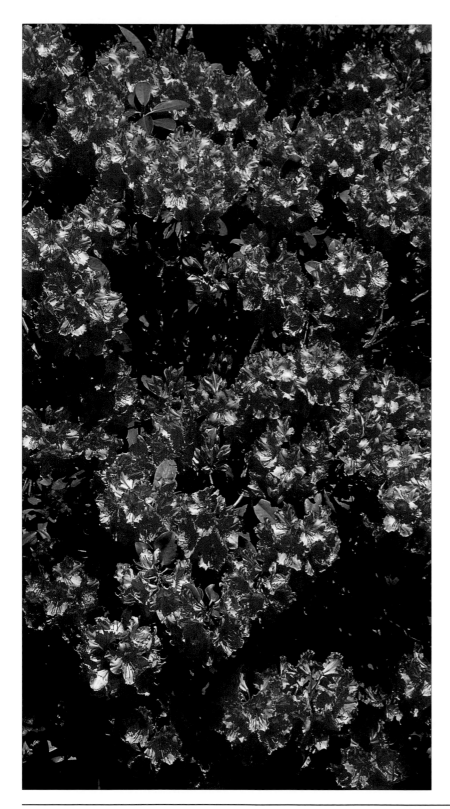

Above: *Forsythia creates one of the biggest splashes of colour in the spring. Here it is used as an informal hedge. It should be cut immediately after flowering to ensure that new flowering shoots grow in time for next season.*

Right: *One of the best-loved spring shrubs is* Magnolia stellata. *Each year it is a mass of delicate star-like flowers in glistening white or tinged with pink. The effect is enhanced because the flowers appear on naked stems, before the leaves develop.*

Left: *Azaleas are a form of rhododendron. There are evergreen and deciduous forms, both producing masses of flowers in a good year. Many of the deciduous forms have a wonderful scent. Like other rhododendrons, they need an acid soil and shelter from hot sun.*

Left: *Berberis are versatile plants, because they are attractive for much of the year: they have spectacular flower displays in spring and good foliage until summer, which then becomes beautifully tinted in the autumn. As an extra, many varieties produce red berries, which often last throughout the winter. Shown here is* Berberis linearifolia *'Orange King'.*

Left: *Lilac* (Syringa) *flowers in the late spring. It has one of the most distinctive smells of all spring-flowering shrubs and is popular for cutting to take indoors. When the flowers die they can look ugly, especially the white forms, and should be removed.*

Above: *A close up of a berberis in flower. This one is* Berberis *'Goldilocks'. Many varieties have sweetly-scented flowers, and all are much loved by bees.*

SPRING-FLOWERING SHRUBS

Berberis	*Magnolia*
Camellia	*Mahonia*
Chaenomeles	*Pieris*
(japonica)	*Prunus* (cherry)
Corylopsis	*Rhododendron*
Corylus (hazel)	*Ribes* (currant)
Cytisus (broom)	*Rosmarinus* (rosemary)
Daphne	*Salix* (willow)
Exochorda	*Spiraea*
Forsythia	*Viburnum*

Shrubs in Summer

While spring is noted for its fresh, young flowers, summer, especially early summer, is the time of mainstream flowering. This is the time for heady scents, particularly on long, warm, summer evenings. It is also a time when insects are at their busiest, with flowering shrubs full of bees and butterflies. Buddleja, in particular, is good for both.

ENJOYING THE SUMMER

Mix in a few summer-flowering shrubs with those from earlier in the year, so that the garden or borders have some form of continuity. Plant fragrant shrubs near where you sit or relax, and use those with thick foliage to create areas of privacy.

There are many types of shrub or dwarf tree that can be used for producing fruit. Currants, gooseberries, cherries, plums and apples can all be grown as small shrubs. These have decorative blossoms in the spring and then provide the delights of picking your own fruit in the summer and autumn. They need not be in a special fruit garden; grow them in ordinary borders, but beware that the soft fruits may

need netting, as they ripen, to prevent birds from eating them.

In a small garden, use large shrubs, rather than trees, to create a shady sitting area. There are many that can be used and they are better suited to being cut to shape than trees.

Generally, there is not much to be done to shrubs during the summer. If the garden is in a town or near a road where there is a lot of dust and grime, wash off the leaves with a sprinkler, or spray if there is a prolonged period of drought, because the film over the surface of the foliage will impair the shrub's ability to make food. Also water, if necessary. Continue to feed those shrubs in containers until the end of the summer.

Above: *In summer the bush* Olearia x haastii *resembles a snowy mountain. Shown in full flower, this one is delicately fronted by a variegated grass,* Phalaris arundinacea *'Picta', more commonly known as "gardener's garters". Always consider the relationship between plants, rather than simply putting them in at random.*

Left: *Roses are at their best in summer. Some are once-flowering and do so in the early summer, but many go on flowering throughout the whole summer. Some gardeners prefer to have a separate garden or special beds for roses, while others like to mix them in with other plants. This lovely old rose is* R. *'Stanwell Perpetual'.*

Above: *From midsummer onwards, the hydrangeas begin to flower. There is a wide range available. The delicate lace-caps are popular because of the shape of the flowers. Here, the beautiful* H. quercifolia, *or oak-leafed hydrangea, combines good flowers and good foliage. Another very attractive hydrangea to consider is* H. aspera *'Villosa', which has soft, furry leaves and subtle, mauvish-blue and pink flowers.*

Above: *Many hydrangeas have white flowers. On the whole, they prefer a shady position and here the whites come into their own, illuminating their surroundings.*

Left: *The vexed question with these mop-headed (*H. macrophylla*) varieties of hydrangea is the colour. The same plant can have blue flowers on acid soil, red ones on a neutral soil and pink ones on an alkaline soil. It is possible to vary the colour by changing the acidity of your soil but, in the long run, it is more satisfactory to go with what you have. If you want to have different colours, plant hydrangeas in containers with the appropriate soil.*

Left: *The rock roses, or* Cistus, *make very fine summer-flowering plants. They are especially good in hot summers as they need a dry soil and can happily cope with droughts. The flowers only last a day, but are replaced by fresh ones the following morning. Some species drop their petals in the early afternoon so they are not much use to the evening gardener. This one is* C. x skanbergii, *with white-centred pink flowers set off against soft, greyish-green foliage.*

Below: *The kalmias are not seen so frequently as they should be. This may be because they need an acid soil and light shade, but even gardeners with alkaline soils should be able to grow them in containers. They flower in early summer, covering the branches with pink or red flowers. These are held in bunches, each flower being cup-shaped in a way that is unique to the plant.*

Above: *Allied to the rock rose, and liking the same kind of hot, dry conditions, are the halimiums. These are evergreen, with white or yellow flowers, some varieties having brown blotches at the base of the petals. This one is* Halimium x pauanum, *a form with pure golden flowers. Again, the flowers are produced afresh each day over a long period through the summer and sometimes well into autumn.*

Above. *The lavateras have become popular with gardeners, and justifiably so. They produce flowers over a long period, from early summer right through to the first frost. Sometimes, after a severe winter, the stems are cut to the ground and, because the new shoots take a time to grow, the flowering does not start until much later in the summer. They are not long-lived plants and it is wise to take cuttings regularly, which is not a difficult task as they root easily.*

Above: *Californian lilacs, Ceanothus, are good-value plants. Although a few of them are deciduous, the majority in cultivation have evergreen foliage that stays attractive throughout the year. In the early summer, they are covered with masses of blue flowers, the shade of blue varying from light to dark, depending on the variety. This is the dwarf form, 'Pin Cushion'.*

Above: *Being closely related, the halimiums and the cistus produce crossbreeds of which this x Halimiocistus revolii is an example. The first part of the name is a combination of those of its parents. This shrub makes a low-spreading carpet of green foliage, which contrasts well with its myriad snow-white flowers.*

Above: *The New Zealand tea tree,* Leptospermum *is becoming increasingly popular, especially in milder areas. They flower over a long period, with masses of small, saucer-shaped flowers in red, pink or white, often with a dark centre. There are also double-flowered varieties and several dwarf forms that are good for rock gardens. This one is* L. scoparium *'Lyndon'.*

Above: *The New Zealand hebes are amongst some of the best summer-flowering plants. They make beautifully-shaped shrubs, with good foliage and masses of flowers that are produced over a long period. The long spikes of flowers seem to whizz around in all directions, like fireworks.*

SUMMER-FLOWERING SHRUBS

Abutilon	*Hydrangea*
Brachyglottis	*Hypericum*
Buddleja	*Indigofera*
Callistemon (bottlebrush)	*Jasminum*
Carpenteria	*Kalmia*
Ceanothus (Californian lilac)	*Lavandula* (lavender)
Cistus (rock rose)	*Lavatera*
Cornus (dog wood)	*Leptospermum*
Deutzia	*Leycesteria*
Erica (heather)	*Olearia* (daisy bush)
Fremontodendron	*Philadelphus* (mock orange)
Fuchsia	*Potentilla*
Halimium	*Rosa*
Hebe	*Sambucus* (elder)
Hibiscus	*Viburnum*
Hoheria	*Weigela*

Above: *Another plant from the same region as the New Zealand hebes is the Australian bottlebrush,* Callistemon. *This shrub has curious bottle-shaped flowers, that explain its common name. Being of Australian origin, they are on the tender side, but some can be brought through to survive most winters by planting against a warm wall. If in doubt, plant in a container and keep inside during the cold months. This species is* C. sieberi.

Right: *Various forms of* Abutilon vitifolium *are appearing in more and more gardens, because it is realized that they are frost hardy. They will not survive a severe winter, but they are quick-growing and can easily be replaced. They come in a range of colours, including red, white and mauve, as here.*

Shrubs in Autumn

Autumn sees the closing of the annual growing cycle. With it come the autumn tints and hues both of the foliage and of the many berries and other fruits. Autumn is the season of reds and browns.

LONG-FLOWERING SHRUBS

There are not many shrubs that flower just in the autumn, but some summer ones continue right through to the frosts. Fuchsias are particularly useful. Buddlejas, hibiscus, hydrangeas, hypericums and indigoferas also continue to flower. One of the true autumn-flowering plants is *Osmanthus heterophyllus*, with its fragrant flowers more reminiscent of spring than of summer. Other plants that are associated with autumn flowering are the ceratostigmas and Eucryphia glutinosa.

AUTUMN LEAVES

The true glory of the autumn belongs to foliage. In a small garden, in particular, it is a wise choice to make every plant earn its keep, and those that provide a fiery end to the year's gardening certainly deserve their place. Berries and other fruit are an added bonus; they are not only attractive but also supply birds and other animals with food for the harsh months ahead.

Autumn is the time to start preparing beds for new planting and indeed to actually start planting. It is also a time to check that those plants that need staking are still securely held in place, before the winter winds begin. Once the leaves have fallen, it is a good idea to go round and examine each shrub, removing any dead or dying wood. Autumn is also the time for clearing up fallen leaves and stopping them from smothering other plants and lawns. Do not waste them by burning or throwing them away. Compost them and return them to the soil once they have rotted.

Right: *While the best-known Osmanthus flower in the spring,* O. heterophyllus *flowers in late autumn, perfuming the air.*

Below: *Hydrangeas are really summer-flowering shrubs, but their flowers last such a long time that they are still flourishing well into autumn, when their leaves lose their green colour and take on autumn tints.*

SHRUBS WITH GOOD AUTUMN FOLIAGE

Amelanchier
Berberis thunbergii
Ceratostigma willmottianum
  (leaves and flowers)
Cotinus (smoke bush)
Enkianthus
Euonymus alatus
Fothergilla
Rhus hirta
Stephandra incisa

SHRUBS WITH GOOD AUTUMN FLOWERS

Buddleja
Ceratostigma
Eucryphia glutinosa
Fuchsia
Hibiscus
Hydrangea
Hypericum
Indigofera
Osmanthus heterophyllus

Above: *The Judas tree is a curious shrub. In spring, purple flowers fill the naked branches; in autumn the leaves take on beautiful colours.*

Left: *Some of the most brilliant of autumn colours are presented by the spindle trees and bushes,* Euonymus. *The colourful* E. alatus *'Compactus' is suitable for the smaller garden. Interest in winter is maintained by its corky wings on the stems.*

Above: *Berberises provide the gardener with a valuable group of plants. They are attractive at all seasons of the year, providing flower, berry and foliage interest. Most produce fiery-coloured foliage and waxy red berries in the autumn, including this* B. thunbergii *'Red Pillar.'*

Above: *Blue is not a colour that one normally associates with the autumn; indeed there are not many shrubs that produce flowers of this colour at any time of year.* Ceratostigma willmottianum *has piercingly blue flowers that carry over from summer well into autumn.*

Right: *Most of the* eucryphias *soon become large trees, but* E. glutinosa, *although it can become large, usually remains small enough to be considered a shrub. The beauty of this plant is the late-season flowers. They are glisteningly white bowls, with a central boss of stamens.*

Left: *As well as its beautiful flowers,* Eucryphia glutinosa *is deciduous, and its leaves take on autumnal tints.*

Above: *Fothergill* (Fothergilla major) *is another good-value shrub with good flowers in late spring or early summer and wonderfully-coloured foliage in autumn. It is very slow growing and although it can eventually become quite large, it will take many years to do so.*

Below: *Many of the cotinus, or smoke bushes, have foliage that is attractive throughout the growing seasons. Many are dark purple, which beautifully set off their smoky plumes of flowers.*

Above: Amelanchier lamarckii *frequently grows into a small tree but, if required, it can be pruned to produce several stems instead of a trunk, so that it becomes a large shrub. It is covered with delicate white flowers in spring and then in autumn its leaves colour beautifully.*

Shrubs in Winter

Winter is often considered the dead month in the garden and many may be tempted to stay indoors. But, in fact, there is a lot going on. A number of shrubs flower at this time of year, some of them with beautiful scents that are particularly noticeable on warm winter days. There are also evergreen shrubs that can look particularly good in the low winter light, especially those with shiny leaves.

WINTER TASKS

There is a lot going on during the winter months and the garden should reflect this. Because many of the shrubs that provide winter interest are dull at other times, they should be planted in less prominent positions. In this way, they will show up in winter when other plants have died back, but will be masked by more interesting plants for the rest of the year.

If the weather is fine and the soil not waterlogged, work can proceed. The more achieved during these winter months, the less there will be to do later in the year. If all the beds are forked over, the weeds removed and the soil mulched, the need for weeding throughout the spring and summer will be considerably reduced. Indeed, one hour spent weeding in winter will save several later on. Provided that the ground is neither waterlogged nor frozen, this is also the best time of year for planting and moving shrubs.

During snowy weather, make certain that shrubs, especially evergreen ones, are not weighed down and broken by excessive falls. Knock the snow off at the earliest opportunity. Light falls should be left if there is a cold wind, because these will help protect the plants.

Above left: *The winter jasmine,* Jasminum nudiflorum, *is truly a winter plant, flowering from the end of autumn through into the early spring, totally ignoring the frost and snow. Stems taken indoors make attractive winter flower decorations.*

Above right: *The winter hazels,* Corylopsis, *make excellent winter plants, with yellow catkins that defy the frosts.*

Right: *Witch hazels,* Hamamelis, *produce curious flowers like clusters of ribbons. As well as being attractive, they have a strident smell that fills the air on sunny days.*

SHRUBS WITH WINTER INTEREST

Corylus (hazel)
Cornus mas (dog wood)
Corylopsis
Hamamelis (witch hazel)
Jasminum nudiflorum
Lonicera purpusii
Lonicera standishii
Lonicera fragrantissima
Mahonia
Viburnum bodnantense
Viburnum farreri
Viburnum tinus

Above and below: *Like many winter-flowering shrubs, the mahonias are beautifully scented. This is possibly to make certain that they attract what few insect pollinators there are at this time of year. Mahonia is a prickly subject and plants can look a bit tatty at some times of year, but in winter it is supreme, with its long spikes of yellow flowers and wafting scent.*

Left: *Viburnums are a versatile group of plants, with at least one variety in flower at each time of year, including two or three in winter. Viburnum tinus is evergreen and is covered with flat heads of flowers throughout most of the winter and often through to the spring as well. On warm days the flowers have a delicate perfume.*

Shrubs with Coloured Stems

Those shrubs that have coloured bark and are grown for their winter stems such as *Rubus cockburnianus, R. thibetanus* and *Salix alba* 'Britzensis' are very worthwhile and are of great value to the winter gardener.

WINTER STEMS

When the leaves have fallen from the shrubs it is time to appreciate what is left: the bare outline of the stems and branches and, more importantly, the colour of the bark. Not all shrubs are coloured in this way but a number provide a wonderful display, especially if they are planted so they catch the low winter sunshine. The shrubs are best cut to the ground each spring, so that there is new growth for the following winter.

SHRUBS WITH COLOURED WINTER STEMS

Cornus alba
Corylus avellana contorta
Rubus cockburnianus
Rubus thibetanus
Salix alba 'Britzensis'

Above: *The red glow of the stems of* Cornus alba *is seen here on a typical winter's day.*

Above: *The ghostly stems of* Rubus cockburnianum *shine out in the winter landscape. The white is a "powdery" bloom, which is lost on older stems, and the whole plant should be cut to the ground each spring to produce new stems for the following winter.*

Above: Cornus stolonifera *'Flaviramea' is quite vibrant with its yellowish green bark. If left to mature, the stems lose their rich colour and hard pruning every spring will ensure plenty of new growth for the following winter.*

Above: Rubus *'Golden Veil' is an extremely attractive plant, with bright yellow foliage in the summer and white stems in the winter. Here the leaves have nearly all fallen, revealing the attractive winter stems beneath.*

Right: *Several of the willows have beautiful winter stems as well as providing their distinctive catkins or pussies at the end of the season.* Salix alba *produces some of the best coloured stems. Here it is represented by* S.a. vitellina *and its variety* S.a.v. 'Britzensis'. *The stems should be cut back each spring to encourage new growth for the following winter.*

Left: *Here* Salix gracilistyla *'Melanostachys' displays the catkins typical of so many willows in the winter. As well as being attractive in the garden, the stems are very popular for adding to indoor winter flower arrangements.*

Plant list

Lists of shrubs for specific purposes (e.g. ground cover) are given in the relevant sections

d = deciduous
e = evergreen

YELLOW-FLOWERED SHRUBS
Azara (e)
Berberis (d & e)
Buddleja globosa (d)
Chimonanthus (d)
Colutea arborescens (d)
Cornus mas (d)
Coronilla (e)
Corylopsis (d)
Corylus (d)
Cytisus (d)
Forsythia (d)
Fremontodendron californicum (e)
Genista (d)
Halimium (e)
Hamamelis (d)
Helianthemum (e)
Hypericum (d)
Jasminum (d & e)
Kerria japonica (d)
Mahonia (e)
Phlomis (e)
Piptanthus (e)
Potentilla (d)
Rhododendron (d & e)
Senecio (d)

Fremontodendron californicum

Azara lanceolata

ORANGE-FLOWERED SHRUBS
Berberis (d & e)
Buddleja x weyeriana (d)
Colutea orientalis (d)
Embothrium coccineum (e)
Helianthemum (e)
Potentilla (d)
Rhododendron (d & e)

Fuchsia 'Genii'

RED-FLOWERED SHRUBS
Callistemon citrinus (e)
Calluna (e)
Camellia (e)
Chaenomeles (d)
Crinodendron hookerianum (e)

Desfontainia spinosa (e)
Erythrina crista-galli (d)
Escallonia (e)
Fuchsia (d)
Helianthemum (e)
Hydrangea (d)
Leptospermum (e)
Rhododendron (d & e)
Ribes speciosum (d)
Weigela (d)

PINK-FLOWERED SHRUBS
Abelia (e)
Andromeda (e)
Buddleja (d)
Calluna (e)
Camellia (e)
Chaenomeles (d)
Cistus (e)

Chaenomeles speciosa 'Moerloosii'

Calluna vulgaris 'Darkness'

Clerodendrum bungei (d)
Cotinus coggygria (d)
Cytisus (d)
Daphne (d & e)
Deutzia (d)
Erica (e)
Escallonia (e)
Fuchsia (d)
Hebe (e)
Helianthemum (e)
Hibiscus (d)
Hydrangea (d)
Indigofera (d)
Kalmia (e)
Kolkwitzia (d)
Lavatera (d)
Leptospermum (e)
Lonicera (d)
Magnolia (d & e)
Nerium (e)
Prunus (d)
Rhododendron (d & e)
Ribes sanguineum (d)
Spiraea (d)
Syringa (d)
Viburnum (d & e)
Weigela (d)

Ceanothus impressus

BLUE-FLOWERED SHRUBS
Buddleja (d)
Caryopteris (d)
Ceanothus (d & e)
Ceratostigma (d)
Hebe (e)
Hibiscus (d)
Hydrangea (d)
Lavandula (e)
Perovskia (d)
Rhododendron (d & e)
Rosmarinus (e)
Vinca (e)

Rhamnus alaternus 'Variegata'
with *Campanula pyramidalis*

Lavandula stoechas (e)
Rhododendron (d & e)
Salvia officinalis (e)
Syringa (d)
Vinca (e)

WHITE-FLOWERED SHRUBS
Aralia (d)
Berberis thunbergia (d)
Buddleja (d)
Calluna (e)
Camellia (e)
Carpenteria californica (e)
Chaenomeles (d)

Syringa vulgaris

PURPLE-FLOWERED SHRUBS
Buddleja (d)
Elsholtzia stauntonii (d)
Erica (e)
Hebe (e)
Hydrangea (d)

Choisya (d)
Cistus (e)
Clerodendrum trichotomum (d)
Clethra alnifolia (d)
Cornus (d)
Cotoneaster (e)
Crataegus (d)
Cytisus (d)
Daphne blagayana (d)
Erica (e)
Escallonia (e)
Eucryphia (d & e)
Exochorda x *macrantha* (d)
Fuchsia (d)
Gaultheria (e)
Halesia (d)
Hebe (e)
Helianthemum (e)
Hibiscus (d)
Hoheria (d)
Hydrangea (d)
Itea (d & e)
Jasminum (d & e)
Leptospermum (e)

Ligustrum (e)
Magnolia (d & e)
Myrtus (e)
Olearia (e)
Osmanthus (e)
Philadelphus (d)
Pieris (e)
Potentilla (d)
Prunus (d)
Pyracantha (e)
Rhododendron (d & e)
Romneya (d)
Rubus 'Tridel' (d)
Sambucus (d)
Skimmia (e)
Spiraea (d)
Stephanandra (d)
Syringa (d)
Viburnum (d & e)
Vinca (e)

GREEN-FLOWERED SHRUBS
Daphne laureola (e)
Garrya elliptica (d)

Carpenteria californica

93

INDEX

Abutilon, 82
  A. megapotamicum
    'Variegatum', 61
  A. vitifolium, 83
Acaena, 44
Acer palmatum
    'Atropurpureum', 56
  A. pseudoplatanus, 24
Aethionema, 50
Allium christophii, 33
Aloysia triphylla, 62
alyssum, 37
Amelanchier, 85
  A. lamarckii, 87
Andromeda, 22, 51
Anemone nemorosa, 38
Arctostaphylos, 30, 51
  A. uva-ursi, 44
ash trees, 24
Astrantia major, 33
Aucuba, 47
  A. japonica, 29
  A.j. 'Crotonifolia', 61
  A.j. 'Mr Goldstrike', 61
  A.j. 'Picturata', 61
Aurinia saxatilis, 37
automatic watering, 22
autumn, 84–7
azaleas, 24, 25, 37, 68, 74, 76
Azara, 64

Ballota pseudodictamnus,
  69
bay, 25
beech, 40, 42
Berberis, 44, 50, 77
  B. darwinii, 24
  B. 'Goldilocks', 77
  B. linearifolia 'Orange
    King', 77
  B. x stenophylla, 64
  B. thunbergii, 85
  B.t. 'Atropurpurea', 56, 57
  B.t. 'Bagatelle', 56
  B.t. 'Red Pillar', 86
  B.t. 'Rose Glow', 33, 61
berries, 66–7, 84
borders: designing, 32–9
  making a new bed, 8–9
bottlebrush, 69, 82, 83
box, 24, 40, 41, 42, 69

Brachyglottis, 82
  B. 'Sunshine', 55
broom, 62, 77
Brunnera macrophylla, 38
Buddleja, 19, 29, 78, 82, 84,
  85
butterfly bush, 29
Buxus, 42
  B. sempervirens, 24, 41, 69

Californian lilac, 81, 82
Callistemon, 82
  C. citrinus, 69
  C. sieberi, 83
Calluna, 22, 30, 44
  C. vulgaris, 44
Camellia, 22, 68, 69, 74, 77
Campanula latifolia, 38
Camphorosma monspeliaca,
  62
cardoons, 39
Carpenteria, 82
Carpinus betulus, 24, 40, 42
Caryopteris x clandonensis,
  54
  C. x clandonensis
    'Worcester Gold', 61
Cassiope, 22, 47, 51
Ceanothus, 34, 39, 82
  C. 'Pin Cushion', 48, 81
  C. prostratus, 50
Ceratostigma, 84, 85

  C. plumbaginoides, 45
  C. willmottianum, 85, 86
Cercis canadensis 'Forest
  Pansy', 56
Cestrum parqui, 64
Chaenomeles, 66, 77
Chamaecyparis lawsoniana,
  42
  C. obtusa, 50
cherries, 77
Choisya ternata, 24, 64
  C.t. 'Sundance', 53
Christmas roses, 38
Cistus, 44, 62, 82
  C. x skanbergii, 80
Clematis viticella, 74
Clerodendron bungei, 30, 62
Clethra, 64
clipping hedges, 42–3
colour, 36–7
  foliage, 54–61
  stems, 90–1
compost, 8
composts, potting, 27, 70
conifers, 52
  dwarf, 49
  hedges, 41, 43
  prostrate, 44
  woodland beds, 51
containers, 68–71
Convallaria majalis, 38
Convolvulus cneorum, 24,
  50, 54, 69

C. sabatius, 50
coppicing, 54
Cordyline australis, 69
  C.a. 'Atropurpurea', 56
Cornus, 29, 82
  C. alba, 30, 90
  C.a. 'Elegantissima', 58
  C.a. 'Sibirica', 37
  C.a. 'Spaethii', 61
  C. alternifolia 'Argentea',
    58
  C. canadensis, 30, 47
  C. controversa 'Variegata',
    58
  C. mas, 88
  C.m. 'Aureoelegantissima',
    59, 69
  C. 'Sibirica', 19
  C. stolonifera 'Flaviramea',
    90
Corylopsis, 64, 77, 88
Corylus, 57, 77, 88
  C. avellana, 24, 41
  C.a. contorta, 90
  C. maxima 'Purpurea', 56
Cotinus, 19, 54, 57, 85, 87
  C. coggygria, 6
  C.c. 'Royal Purple', 33, 56
Cotoneaster, 44, 66, 67, 69
  C. simonsii, 24
cotton lavender, 55
Crataegus, 42, 66
  C. monogyna, 24, 41
crossing stems, pruning, 18
x Cupressocyparis leylandii,
  24, 40, 42
currants, 29, 74, 77
cuttings, 28–9
Cyclamen hederifolium, 38
Cynara cardunculus, 39
Cytisus, 62, 77

daisy bush, 69, 82
Daphne, 50, 51, 64, 66, 77
  D. x burkwoodii
    'Somerset', 33, 64
  D. x burkwoodii 'Somerset
    Gold Edge', 61
  D. tangutica, 51
dead-heading, 19
dead wood, pruning, 16, 18
designing borders, 32–9

Deutzia, 82
Dictamnus albus purpureus,
  33
die-back, pruning, 18
Digitalis purpurea, 33
division, 30
dogwood, 19, 29, 47, 82, 88
droughts, 24
Dryas octopetala, 50
dwarf shrubs, 48–51

Elaeagnus, 64
  E. x ebbingei, 24
  E. 'Quicksilver', 36, 54, 55
elder, 19, 29, 54, 60, 62, 65,
  68, 82
Enkianthus, 22, 85
Eranthis hyemalis, 38
Erica, 30, 44, 50, 51, 69, 82
ericaceous plants, 22
Eryngium giganteum, 33
Erysimum 'Bowles Mauve',
  36
Escallonia 'Gwendolyn
  Anley', 9
  E. 'Langleyensis', 24
Eucalyptus, 39
Eucryphia glutinosa, 84, 85,
  86
Euonymus, 44, 47
  E. alatus, 85
  E.a. 'Compactus', 85
  E. europaeus, 66
  E. fortunei, 44
  E.f. 'Emerald Gaiety', 58, 68
  E.f. 'Emerald 'n' Gold', 44
  E.f. 'Gold Spot', 61
  E.f. 'Sunshine', 61
  E.f. 'Variegatus', 58
  E. japonicus 'Aureopictus',
    61
  E.j. 'Macrophyllus', 24
  E.j. 'Microphyllus
    Variegatus', 58
  E. nana, 50
Euphorbia amygdaloides
  robbiae, 38
Euryops acreus, 50
evergreens, 52–3
Exochorda, 77
  E. x macrantha 'The Bride',
    75

Fagus sylvatica, 40, 42
  F.s. 'Riversii', 56
fertilizers, 23, 70
firethorn, 24, 41, 66
flowers: autumn, 84–6
  fragrant, 64–5
  spring, 74–7
  summer, 78–83
  winter, 89
foliage: autumn, 84–7
  coloured, 54–61
  evergreens, 52–3
  fragrant, 62–3
Forsythia, 29, 76, 77
Fothergilla, 85
  F. major, 87
fragrance: flowers, 64–5
  foliage, 62–3
Fraxinus excelsior, 24
Fremontodendron, 82
frost, 24, 25, 74
fruit, 66–7, 78, 84
Fuchsia, 69, 82, 84, 85
  F. magellanica 'Variegata', 58
  F. procumbens, 50

Galanthus, 38
Gaultheria, 22, 30, 47, 51, 68
  G. mucronata, 66
Genista lydia, 48, 50
Geranium, 38, 39
  G. x *oxonianum,* 59
  G. sanguineum, 49
gravel beds, 50
Griselinia littoralis, 24
ground cover, 44–7

x *Halimiocistus revolii,* 48, 50, 81
Halimium, 82
  H. x *pauanum,* 80
Hamamelis, 64, 88
hawthorn, 24, 41, 42, 66
hazel, 24, 41, 57, 77, 88
heather, 22, 44, 50, 51, 68, 69, 82
Hebe, 50, 69, 82
  H. cupressoides, 53, 63
  H. pinguifolia 'Pagei', 44, 54
Hedera, 44, 47

hedges, 24, 40–3
Helianthemum, 49, 50, 69
  H. 'Wisley Pink', 55
Helleborus, 38
Hibiscus, 82, 84, 85
Hippophaë rhamnoides, 24, 54, 66
Hoheria, 82
holly, 24, 41, 42, 66, 67, 69, 72
Holodiscolor, 30
honeysuckle, box-leaf, 24, 42, 72
hornbeam, 24, 40, 42
Hydrangea, 22, 69, 82, 84, 85
  H. aspera 'Villosa', 79
  H. 'Ayesha', 17
  H. macrophylla, 79
  H. quercifolia, 79
Hypericum, 46, 50, 69, 82, 84, 85
  H. calycinum, 44

Ilex, 24, 42, 66, 69, 72
  I. x *altaclerensis* 'Golden King', 61
  I. x *altaclerensis* 'Lawsoniana', 61
  I. aquifolium, 41
  I.a. 'Aurifodina', 61
  I.a. 'Crispa Aureopicta', 61
  I.a. 'Ferox Argentea', 67
  I.a. 'Golden Milkboy', 61
Indigofera, 69, 82, 84, 85
Itea, 64
ivy, 44, 46, 47

japonica, 66, 77
Jasminum, 82
  J. nudiflorum, 88
judas tree, 85
Juniperus (juniper), 52, 62
  J. communis 'Compressa', 48, 49, 50
  J.c. 'Prostrata', 44
  J. sabina tamariscifolia, 44
  J. squamata 'Blue Carpet', 44

Kalmia, 22, 51, 69, 80, 82
Kalmiopsis, 51
Kerria, 30

laurel, 42, 43, 62, 69
  cherry, 24
  Portuguese, 24, 42
  spotted, 29
Laurus nobilis, 25, 62, 69
Laurustinus, 24
Lavandula (lavender), 24, 40, 41, 42, 62, 68, 69, 82
  L. angustifolia, 54
  L. stoechas, 34
  L.s. pedunculata, 36
Lavatera, 81, 82
Lawson's cypress, 42
layering, 30–1
leaves see foliage
Leptospermum, 82
  L. scoparium 'Lyndon', 82
  L.s. 'Nanum', 50
Leucothoe, 30
Leycesteria, 82
leyland cypress, 24, 40, 42
Ligustrum, 29, 42, 66, 72
  L. lucidum 'Excelsum Superbum', 52
  L. ovalifolium, 24
  L.o. 'Aureum', 61
lilac, 25, 77
lily-of-the-valley, 38
Lithodora diffusa, 37, 44, 45, 50
Lonicera fragrantissima, 88
  L. nitida, 24, 42, 72
  L. pileata, 47
  L. purpusii, 88
  L. pyrenaica, 50
  L. standishii, 88
Lychnis chalcedonica, 38
  L. coronaria 'Alba', 33

Magnolia, 64, 74, 77
  M. stellata, 76
Mahonia, 30, 64, 77, 88, 89
Mexican orange-blossom, 64
Micromeria corsica, 50
mock orange, 29, 64, 65, 82
moving shrubs, 12–13
mulching, 11, 21
Myrica, 62
Myrtus (myrtle), 62, 64, 69
  M. communis, 62, 69

Nandina, 30
New Zealand flax, 69

Olearia, 34, 69, 82
  O. x *haastii,* 78
Ononis, 50
organic matter, 8
Osmanthus, 64
  O. heterophyllus, 84, 85
  O.h. 'Goshiki', 61

Pachysandra, 30, 47
  P. terminalis, 44
Papaver somniferum, 33
periwinkle, 44, 45, 47
pernettya, 51, 66
Perovskia, 62
  P. atriplicifolia 'Blue Spire', 33
Phalaris arundinacea 'Picta', 78
Philadelphus, 29, 64, 65, 82
Phormium, 69
  P. cookianum, 33
Phyllodoce, 22, 51
Picea sitchensis, 24
Pieris, 22, 68, 71, 74, 77
  P. japonica, 53
Pinus sylvestris, 24
Piptanthus, 66
Pittosporum laurocerasus, 24
plans, 32
planting shrubs, 10–11

containers, 70–1
gravel beds, 50
ground cover, 46–7
hedges, 42
moving shrubs, 12–13
pollarding, 54
Polygonatum, 38
Potentilla, 21, 82
  P. fruticosa, 44
pricking out, 27
Primula, 38
privet, 24, 42, 52, 72
propagation: cuttings, 28–9
  division, 30
  layering, 30–1
  seeds, 26–7
Prostanthera cuneata, 34, 62
pruning, 16–19
  roots, 12
Prunus, 77
  P. cerasifera 'Nigra', 56
  P. x *cistena,* 56
  P. laurocerasus, 42, 43
  P. lusitanica, 24, 42
  P.l. 'Variegata', 58
purple foliage, 56–7
Pyracantha, 24, 41, 66
Pyrus salicifolia 'Pendula', 54

reversion, variegated foliage, 59

Rhamnus alaternus
  'Argenteovariegata', 58, 59
Rhododendron, 22, 24, 31,
  34, 38, 44, 47, 51, 53, 68,
  69, 74, 75, 77
  R. luteum, 64
Rhus hirta, 85
Ribes, 29, 77
  R. sanguineum, 74
rock gardens, 48, 49, 50
rock roses, 44, 49, 62, 80,
  82
roots: layering, 30–1
  moving shrubs, 12–13
  planting shrubs, 11
  wind rock, 14
Rosa (roses), 29, 39, 40, 62,
  64, 66, 69, 82
  R. glauca, 19, 54
  R. 'Miss Pam Ayres', 19
  R. pimpinellifolia, 67
  R. rubiginosa 'Lady
    Penzance', 62
  R. 'Stanwell Perpetual', 78
  R. 'Wenlock Castle', 33
  R. 'Zéphirine Drouhin',
    65
Rosmarinus (rosemary), 24,
  62, 63, 69, 77
  R. officinalis, 24
rowan, 24
Rubus, 30
  R. cockburnianus, 19, 90
  R. 'Golden Veil', 91
  R. thibetanus, 90

sage, 60, 62, 63
Salix, 19, 29, 77
  S. alba vitellina, 91
  S.a.v. 'Britzensis', 54, 90, 91
  S. gracilistyla
    'Melanostachys', 91
  S. helvetica, 49, 50
  S. lanata, 54
  S. repens, 37, 44, 45, 50
Salvia forsskaolii, 33
  S. officinalis, 62
  S.o. 'Icterina', 60
  S.o. 'Purpurascens', 36, 56
  S. sclarea, 39
Sambucus, 19, 29, 54, 62, 82
  S. nigra, 61
  S. racemosa 'Plumosa
    Aurea', 60, 68
Santolina, 62
  S. chamaecyparis, 54, 55
  S. pinnata neapolitana, 54
Sarcococca, 30, 47, 64
saws, pruning, 16
Scots pine, 24
sea buckthorn, 24
secateurs (pruners), 16, 17
Sedum spectabile
  'September Glow', 33
seedlings, pricking out, 27
seeds, sowing, 26–7
silver foliage, 54–5, 58
sitka spruce, 24
Skimmia, 64, 66, 67, 69
smoke bush, 19, 54, 57, 85,
  87

snow, 88
snowdrops, 38
soil: conditioners, 8
  planting shrubs, 10–11
  preparation, 8–9
  woodland beds, 51
Sorbus aucuparia, 24
  S. reducta, 30, 50
Spiraea, 29, 58, 77
  S. 'Arguta', 11, 74
  S. japonica 'Goldflame', 23,
    59
spring, 74–7
sprinklers, 22
spurge, wood, 38
Stachys byzantina, 33
staking, 14–15
stems, colour, 37, 90–1

Stephandra incisa, 44, 85
summer, 78–83
supports, 14–15
sweet box, 64
sycamore, 24
Symphoricarpos, 66
Syringa, 25, 77

Tamarix, 24
Taxus, 42
  T. baccata, 24, 40
tea tree, New Zealand, 82
Teucrium, 50
Thuja plicata, 42
Thymus (thyme), 50, 62
ties, staking shrubs, 14–15
topiary, 72–3
transplanting shrubs, 12–13

Vaccinium, 22, 47, 51, 68
variegated foliage, 54, 58–61
Verbascum 'Letitia', 50
Viburnum, 29, 77, 82
  V. bodnantense, 88
  V. farreri, 88
  V. x *juddii*, 65
  V. opulus, 66
  V. tinus, 24, 88, 89
Vinca, 47
  V. minor, 44, 45, 47
  V.m. 'Argenteovariegata',
    58

watering, 22
weather, 24–5
weeds, 8, 20–1, 46, 88
Weigela, 82
  W. florida 'Albomarginata',
    58
  W.f. 'Florida Variegata', 33
  W.f. 'Foliis Purpurea', 56
willow, 19, 29, 37, 49, 77,
  91
wind, 14, 24
winter, 24, 25, 88–91
witch hazel, 64, 88
wood anemones, 38
woodland plants, 38, 51

yellow, variegated foliage,
  61
yew, 24, 40, 42, 73
Yucca, 69
  Y. gloriosa 'Variegata', 33

ACKNOWLEDGEMENTS

The publishers would like to thank the following for their permission to photograph their plants and gardens: Hilary and Richard Bird, Ken Bronwin, Mr and Mrs R. Cunningham, Chris and Stuart Fagg, Della and Colin Fox, Merriments Gardens, Eric Pierson, the RHS Garden Wisley, Mavis and David Seeney, Lyn and Brian Smith.

They would also like to thank the following people for allowing their pictures (to which they own the copyright) to be reproduced in this book:
Jonathan Buckley for the pictures on p.17 (b), p.45 (br), p.51 (tr), p.51 (br), p.67 (tr), p.67 (bl), p.67 (br), p.76 (tr), p.84 (b), p.85 (r), p.87 (l), p.88 (br), p.89 (br), p.89 (l), p.90 (all), p.91 (all);
The Garden Picture Library for the picture on p.34; Derek St Romaine for the picture on p.33;
Peter McHoy for the pictures on p.19 (tr), p.24, p.25 (br), p.37 (tl), p.43 (br), p.61 (tr), p.66 (tr), p.66 (br), p.67 (tr), p.74 (tl), p.74 (tr), p.76 (br), p.77 (bl), p.84 (tr), p.85 (l), p.86 (all), p.87 (tr), p.87 (br), p.88 (tl), p.88 (tr), p.89 (br), p. 92 (bl), p.92 (tc), p.92 (bc), p.93 (t), p.93 (br), p.95.

Key: t = top; b = bottom; r = right; l = left; c = centre